M000213187

# THE HAINDL
# TAROT

## VOLUME II:
## THE MINOR ARCANA

BOOKS BY RACHEL POLLACK

# THE HAINDL
# TAROT

## VOLUME II:
## THE MINOR ARCANA

## RACHEL POLLACK

NEWCASTLE PUBLISHING, INC.
NORTH HOLLYWOOD, CALIFORNIA
1990

Originally published as *Der Haindl Tarot*
Copyright © 1988 by Rachel Pollack
Copyright © 1988 für die Karten by Droemersche Verlagsanstalt
   Th. Knaur Nachf., München
Droemer Knaur, 1988

Copyright © 1990 by Rachel Pollack
All rights reserved.
ISBN 8-87877-156-5

Edited by J. Kelley Younger
Copyedited by Ann McCarthy
Haindl Tarot illustrations by Hermann Haindl
Cover Design by Michele Lanci-Altomare

No part of this book may be reproduced in any form without the express
written consent of the publisher, except by a reviewer, who may quote brief
passages in connection with a review.

Illustrations of the Minor Arcana from the Haindl Tarot Deck are
reproduced herein through the permission of U.S. Games Systems, Inc.

This book is not intended to diagnose, prescribe or treat any ailment, nor
is it intended in any way as a replacement for medical consultation when
needed. The author and publishers of this book do not guarantee the effi-
cacy of any methods herein described, and strongly suggest that at the first
suspicion of any disease or disorder the reader consult a physician.

FIRST EDITION
A NEWCASTLE BOOK
First printing, 1990
10  9  8  7  6  5  4
Printed in the United States of America

*Dedicated to Tana Dineen*

# Contents

# FOREWORD

Artistic vision registers and prophesies the expanding consciousness of man. I am not speaking only of works of art, but the artistic vision wherever it imbues living acts. Artistic imagination creates what has never before existed. To live artistically is to embody in social forms the unique individual and the intuitions of union.

—M. C. Richards

THE HAINDL TAROT captures the essence of artistic vision and honors the true meaning of the word *craft* which comes from the German word *Kraft,* meaning power and strength. The collaborative team of Rachel Pollack, award-winning writer, and visionary artist Hermann Haindl demonstrates the power and strength of two people committed to the combined craft of Tarot.

Artful in their respective crafts, Pollack and Haindl live with a special immediacy to the questions of technique and the questions of meaning and how they apply to Tarot. Through art, Haindl addresses the questions of technique; and through writing, Pollack addresses meaning. Using different means to achieve a combined result, Pollack and Haindl illustrate how perennial and ancient wisdoms can be applied in contemporary times. Haindl, through his contemporary style and Tarot deck, renders traditional archetypes with modern symbols. Pollack skillfully interprets the many layers of meanings found within the symbols. She brings together multiple spiritual and esoteric traditions and demonstrates their relevance and varied applications in modern themes of ecology, politics and ways of developing human resources.

The Haindl Tarot and Rachel Pollack's interpretations reveal the power of the creative arts in their capacity to bridge visible and invisible worlds. The rich matrix of the Tarot provides a symbolic map of consciousness which can serve as a visual affirmation and a synchronistic mirror of an individual's experience and life process. Combining the oracular traditions of the *I-Ching,* Runes, astrology and the influence of ancient cultures and the Kabbalah, these two volumes synthesize multiple doorways in which mainstream people and scholars can access invaluable information.

The challenge of the twenty-first century is how to integrate ancient and modern themes that will create synergetic visions and applications which can further the expanding consciousness of humankind. Perhaps Cezanne described this process best when he said: "Any craft is a harmony parallel to nature." Rachel Pollack and the Haindl Tarot remind us that symbols provide a harmonious mirror of our own nature and craft; and that it is time, as M. C. Richards states, "to live artistically . . . to embody in social forms the unique individual and the intuitions of union." In many ways, Pollack and Haindl have paved the way in their joint effort in bringing forward the Haindl Tarot.

Angeles Arrien
San Francisco, California
Spring 1990

# AUTHOR'S PREFACE

THE WORD "TAROT" is a French word for a card game known also as "Tarocchi" or "Tarock." Nobody really knows the Tarot's origin. Many people have put forth theories, some of them mundane, others esoteric or frankly legendary. At one end of the scale we find the idea that the Tarot began simply as a game with no deeper meaning until occultists invented fantasies about it in the eighteenth century. At the other end we read of secret congregations of Atlantean masters who wanted to encode their wisdom for the dark ages after Atlantis's destruction. As far as historical information tells us, the Tarot first appeared in Italy in the mid-fifteenth century. Contrary to what we might expect, cards of any kind do not get mentioned in European documents until the late fourteenth century. Among the earliest cards that have come down to us are the Tarot cards painted by Bonifacio Bembo for the aristocratic Visconti family of Italy.

The Tarot has remained remarkably the same throughout its history. From the time of Bembo the deck has consisted of seventy-eight cards ("seventy-eight degrees of wisdom," as Charles Williams called them), in two main parts, referred to by esotericists as the Major Arcana and the Minor Arcana (*arcana* means "secrets"). The Major Arcana are twenty-two trump cards, usually numbered 0–21 and displaying names, such as "The Empress" or "The Fool." The Minor Arcana contain four suits of fourteen cards each, ace through ten and four "court" cards: page, knight, queen, king.

Though the structure has stayed the same, the pictures on the cards have changed a great deal. The images most people think of as traditional, or classic, the images found on the famous Tarot de Marseille, became fixed fairly early, around the seventeenth century. Nevertheless, many of them vary quite strongly from the pictures left to us by Bembo. People who know the Tarot may look at the cards created by Hermann Haindl with some surprise, for he has radically redesigned almost all the images. And yet, we can consider such alteration as part of the Tarot's tradition. Interestingly, the card that remains closest to the older decks is the famous Hanged Man.

This same card probably has varied the least throughout the Tarot's many transformations.

Many people have put forth esoteric theories of the Tarot's origin (see also the introduction to the Major Arcana). The fact remains that as far as we know, the occult interest in the Tarot did not begin until the late-eighteenth century when a man named Antoine Court de Gebelin declared that the Tarot formed the "Book of Thoth," a supposed compilation of ancient Egyptian wisdom created by the God Thoth for his disciple magicians. In Classical times people considered Thoth the equivalent of the Greek Hermes, or Roman Mercury. Hermes' name has been given to the "Hermetic," or esoteric tradition. In the correspondence of the Tarot trumps to astrology, the planet (and god) Mercury belongs to the card of the Magician. Following Court de Gebelin, various people began to create occult Tarot decks. The most important of these was the Grand Etteilla deck, "Etteilla" simply being the artist's name, Alliette, spelled backwards.

Probably the most significant development for the Tarot came in the mid-nineteenth century, when the occultist Eliphas Levi (whose real name was Alphonse Louis Constant), connected the Tarot to the body of Jewish mysticism known as Kabbalah (a word which means tradition). Ever since the Middle Ages Kabbalistic ideas had fertilized the wider Hermetic and magical philosophies. By noticing a remarkable correlation between the Kabbalah's structure and that of the Tarot (see the Major Arcana introduction) Levi set the Tarot in a direction that has remained important to this day.

In 1888 a man named MacGregor Mathers, who had written about the Tarot and fortune-telling, joined with others to found the Hermetic Order of the Golden Dawn. This organization continued for only a few decades but its influence remains strong today. It carried Levi's ideas further, formulating complex correspondences bewteen the Tarot, Kabbalah, astrology and ceremonial magic. It also led to people using the cards as aids in study, meditation and ritual. The Golden Dawn urged its members to create their own decks based on the group's doctrines. This idea of individual creation may have helped foster the modern renaissance in Tarot, with literally hundreds of new decks, many of them vastly different from earlier designs.

Apart from the poet William Butler Yeats, the two most famous members of the Golden Dawn were Arthur Edward Waite and

Aleister Crowley. Both designed their own Tarot decks. The one by Waite, known as the Rider deck (after its London publisher), and painted by Pamela Colman Smith, has become the world's most popular deck, probably because of Smith's vivid images. Crowley's Book of Thoth Tarot went further than most other decks in directly incorporating esoteric and sexual symbolism. Because of this—and because of the stunning pictures painted by Lady Frieda Harris— the Book of Thoth has influenced a great many Tarot artists of the last forty years. One of these is Hermann Haindl, who consulted Crowley as a source when he decided to paint his own cards.

Though the Haindl Tarot contains much esoteric information, including Hebrew letters, Runes, astrological symbols and *I Ching* hexagrams, we should not think of it as an occult deck, not in the sense of Crowley. We do not find here the precise details of Hermetic symbolism, the references to doctrines and rituals, the complex use of magical signs and formulas coded into the pictures. Rather than an occult work, Hermann Haindl has created a *sacred* Tarot, one which reaches back to ancient spiritual traditions of many cultures.

The Haindl Tarot certainly contains a great deal of information. Most importantly, however, it opens our minds. It leads us to see the world in a new way (or perhaps a very old way), as a vessel filled with spiritual power and truth. To do this, the deck does indeed draw on Crowley and other representatives of the Tarot's occult teachings. It also draws on the mythologies and the religions of different peoples, from Europe to Native America, to India, to China, to Egypt. And it takes inspiration from sacred art, from prehistoric statues and temples to Wagnerian opera. None of these things becomes a doctrine, not in the narrow sense of a fixed ideology. As an artist, Hermann seeks to create an inner understanding rather than promulgate a particular theory.

The deck certainly does contain ideas. Though Hermann Haindl worked to a large extent unconsciously—not planning the symbolism so much as allowing it to emerge in the painting—the pictures present to us a complex and, at the same time, unified vision. We will explore this vision and its concepts in the individual cards. Here, we can describe the central theme of the Haindl Tarot as the renewal of the Earth—not just the material resources, but the spiritual Earth. For thousands of years people have seen the Earth as a living being. All over the world She was worshipped as an aspect

of the Great Goddess, the Mother of Life. The Goddess is the
Earth, and She is also the Sky. She rules as well over the mythological realms of Heaven and the Underworld.

In recent years we have become conscious of two great dangers
facing our world. One is the possibility of nuclear war ending all life
in the fire of explosions and the darkness of nuclear winter. The
other is the threat to our planet's environment. Various groups,
including the Green Party in Germany, have attempted to push for
disarmament, as well as to stop the acid rain, the cutting down of
forests, the destruction of the ozone layer of the atmosphere. Hermann Haindl, like many others, sees this as a spiritual struggle as
well as an ecological and political one. For Haindl, the roots of our
current dangers originate in a male-dominated mentality, one based
on hierarchies and dominance, rather than cooperation and mutual
respect. When patriarchal ideologies banished the Goddess, women
became seen as primarily vehicles for producing babies—and the
Earth became an object rather than a Creator, an object created
solely for human exploitation. Hermann Haindl is not a feminist.
Nor does the Haindl Tarot attack men. Rather, it seeks a balance
between different qualities. And it roots this balance in the ancient
view of the female as the primary principle of creation.

Though Haindl has worked in the Green Party, he has come to
his ideas more through his own experience, primarily with the native peoples of North America. Hermann Haindl and his wife, Erica
Haindl, have traveled among the Native Americans; they have
stayed in their homes and taken part in their rituals. They did not
go to the Native Americans out of curiosity. They went to learn, and
to awaken in themselves a genuine respect for the Earth and for the
Spirits who share our world.

The Haindl Tarot does not spell out Native American teachings
any more than it does occult doctrines. Haindl's American experiences form an influence in the deck, along with his travels in India
and other lands, his knowledge of European mythology and traditions and the Tarot itself. Above all, he has created a sacred work
of art, one which speaks to us through the power of its images.

At one time, the symbolism in a Tarot deck counted more than
the pictures. People concerned themselves less with the quality of
the art and more with specific references to some teaching, such as
Kabbalah or Freemasonry. This may help to explain why relatively

few professional artists have created Tarot decks. Perhaps the subject struck them as too restricted, even for those with esoteric interests. In recent years, however, the vast number of new decks have returned the image to a primal place. The Haindl Tarot re-works the old designs in a radical way, but it does not do so alone. Other people have begun to re-imagine the Tarot, creating new pictures out of their own lives and beliefs. The strongest of these pictures have gone beyond the personal to archaic and mythological levels. We find this kind of power in the Haindl Tarot, especially in such cards as the Chariot, or the Star, or the very beautiful Court cards, derived from religious traditions around the world. Once again, trained artists have begun to explore the Tarot. Along with such figures as Salvador Dali and Niki de St. Phalle, a whole group of young artists, particularly in Italy, the home of Tarocchi, have created their own decks. The Haindl Tarot goes deeper than most, for it forms the life testament of an artist dedicated to spiritual understanding.

The Haindl cards are obviously symbolic. Each card, but especially those of the Major Arcana, contains an entire structure of symbolism, based on a set of ideas and images derived from tradition, but finally belonging to this particular deck. Because Haindl is first and foremost a painter, the meanings become part of the picture, rather than the picture being formed only to serve a theory. Many cards show what we might term an "economy of symbolism." A single gesture, or an object, or a color pattern, will appear simple, but will actually convey a whole range of ideas. These ideas then create a new relationship with each other. The card has brought them together. We find this technique in many of the trumps, notably the Fool, but also in the Minor Suit and Court cards.

I first heard of the Haindl Tarot when Hermann Haindl's German publisher called me on the telephone to ask if I would like to write a commentary for a new deck. I asked him to send me some of the pictures. The moment they arrived they struck me with their conceptual beauty, their daring designs and their sense of mystery. I had recently done some writing on the Runes, so it seemed to me a wonderful idea to bring this ancient system into the Major Arcana. Shortly afterwards, I met Hermann and Erica Haindl for the first time. They came to my house in Amsterdam, arms laden with paintings, and we sat for several hours, looking at the cards, talking about the symbolism, discovering the many ways in which we all shared the same concepts—of the Tarot, of politics, of mythology and archaic beliefs. When they left they gave me a kachina doll, a sacred image to bring favor to the house. In return, I gave them a rock I had found containing a natural Rune. The next time I saw them, in their home in Germany, they presented me with a rock from a beach in Tuscany. The rock had a six-pointed star etched by nature into its surface; Hermann had searched among the pebbles on the beach until he found one containing an appropriate symbol.

In describing these cards I have attempted to follow Hermann Haindl's statements as closely as possible. At the same time I have brought to them my own ideas and experiences, not to contradict the message in the pictures, but to explore them and their possibilities. Hermann Haindl and I come from different cultures, different generations, different genders, different religious backgrounds, different creative disciplines. Yet we can experience the world in a similar way. Working with the Haindl Tarot has taught me a great deal. I hope that this book will enable others to enter this new and ancient labyrinth.

Rachel Pollack

# THE NUMBERED CARDS

# Introduction to the Minor Arcana Numbered Cards

THE MINOR ARCANA are most likely the ancestor of modern playing cards (just as Tarocchi is probably the ancestor of bridge and other trump games). The four suits comprise fourteen cards each, ace through ten, and four Court cards. In most Tarot decks the Court cards are similar to ordinary playing cards, with the addition of a knight to make the quartet—page, knight, queen and king. The Haindl Tarot (as well as some other contemporary Tarot decks) has greatly changed the Court cards, in effect making them a separate group. Therefore, we will look at them in their own section. This section, then—the Minor Arcana numbered cards—consists of cards ace through ten in the four suits: Wands, Cups, Swords and Stones.

Another reason for separating the numbered cards from the Court cards in this deck is the method of composition. Hermann Haindl created each of the three sections of the deck in different ways. For the Major Arcana cards, or "trumps,"* he worked almost as a "channeler," allowing the images to emerge in the painting. For the Court cards he followed traditional pictures from different cultures. The numbered cards were done in yet a different way. He first looked through different decks and writers, especially Aleister Crowley, until he decided on the themes each card needed to express. These became the titles of the cards. Once he knew the title, he looked through his own past work, finding a particular painting that expressed similar ideas. When he had found the appropriate painting, he would look it over very carefully and choose a single part that most depicted the theme, whether it was love, endangered nature or any of the others. He then photographed this detail for the card's background.

This method gives the deck continuity. It ties this important project to all of Haindl's previous work over many years. It also links

---

*For all references to the Major Arcana cards throughout this work see *The Haindl Tarot, Volume I.*

the cards with each other, for some paintings provide details for several cards. Sometimes these are all in the same suit, such as the painting *Kathedrale* for the Two, Three, Four, and Nine of Wands. At other times they cross the suits, such as the picture used for the Seven of Wands, the Ten of Cups and the Six of Stones. In this way the ideas and the different suits move in and out of each other.

With the background established, Haindl added the symbols—four cups for the Four of Cups, six swords for the Six of Swords, and so on. He did this in the best way to further express what the card needed to say. For some, such as the Six of Cups, the picture dictated the arrangement of the symbols. For others, he chose a pattern that went with the theme. This might be orderly for a card expressing balance or community, or no pattern at all for a card showing chaos.

In a sense, Haindl worked backwards, from the title to the background to the foreground. By working out the themes first, he gives the cards a certain objective quality. The titles have sent him in particular directions. The Two of Stones has to express "Harmony," the Five of Swords "Defeat." It then becomes a question of the best way to show this. This method also helps link the Haindl Tarot to Tarot tradition.

Even though the backgrounds come from older works we should not consider these as separate from the symbols. The placing of the symbols changes the backgrounds so that they become new pictures. The cards have a dreamlike quality. This comes partly from the fantastic imagery in many of the backgrounds, but also from the way the Cups or Stones float in front, while the Swords pierce the pictures and the spears (Wands) rise out of the background.

There are few human beings in these cards—mostly animals, plants, rock, water and ruined buildings. Hermann Haindl has said he created these cards for nature. At the same time, the images and symbols teach us about ourselves. This follows the ancient tradition of fables, like the stories of Aesop or La Fontaine, where animals act out lessons. It follows the philosophy of Transcendentalism (itself derived partly from Native American tradition), in which all nature matches qualities in the human soul.

In most Tarot decks the Major cards show spiritual qualities and the Minor cards represent aspects of daily life—relationships, work, emotions, money and so on. While the Haindl Tarot follows this pattern, it does not restrict the Minor cards to individual experience.

Haindl describes his Minor cards as "communal." We see this very much in the Swords and Stones. The Swords symbolize people's conflicts, but they also reflect political problems in society. The Stones also deal with social issues. The Three of Stones, "Work," traditionally indicates a single person at work. Haindl has broadened this to deal with questions of unemployment and meaningless jobs. And beyond the communal aspects, the cards, especially the Stones, bring us back to the basic issues we saw in the Major Arcana.

The Minor cards are divided into four suits, Wands, Cups, Swords and Stones. In older Tarot decks Wands were often Staves, and Stones were usually coins or disks. In the twentieth century this last suit became Pentacles. Those who see the original Tarot as a card game, based on medieval social structures, view the suits as the four main social classes and their tools. Peasants grew sticks (wands), priests held chalices (cups), noblemen fought with swords, and merchants traded in money (coins). People who view the Tarot in more esoteric terms usually point out the connection of the four symbols with the Holy Grail. In many of the Grail stories we find a ritual in which a maiden carries the Grail, a cup, on a disk, while other maidens carry a sword and a spear. Esotericists also point out the importance of these objects in ritual magic, with an actual wand used by the magician, and a pentacle replacing the coin.

Whatever their origins, the four suits have come to signify different areas of life. Roughly speaking, Wands represent action and excitement, Cups love and imagination, Swords conflict and intellect, and Coins (Stones) work and nature. We can also describe the phallic Wands and Swords as masculine, and the Cups and Stones as feminine. We can substitute the Chinese terms *yang* and *yin* for masculine and feminine. These distinctions do not create strict barriers. We can make different divisions as well. Wands and Cups look at life optimistically. They represent light (yang). Swords and Stones, but especially Swords, take a darker view (yin), though here the Stones end as the most optimistic. Also, Wands and Stones signify outer concerns, such as work, while Cups and Swords deal with emotions. Each suit can join with any of the others.

The primary symbolic idea for the four suits is that of the four elements, Fire, Water, Air and Earth. These belong to Wands, Cups, Swords and Stones. We have already seen this concept of elements with the Major Arcana. Here they give each suit its particular character.

There are other "fours" that give meaning to these cards. For many peoples, but especially the Native Americans, the four directions of the compass carry special qualities. These begin with their natural properties, such as dawn for the east and sunset for the west, cold for the north and warmth for the south. They then become associated with the seasons, particular colors, healing properties, and so on. Those of us who live apart from nature should remember that the seasons are not an arbitrary invention of humans but derive from four special moments in the year: the two solstices and the two equinoxes. These divide the year precisely into quarters.

Carl Jung developed a psychological version of the four elements. Fire becomes Intuition, Water Feeling, Air Thinking, and Earth Sensation. Jung considered these as primary ways people experience the world. Some Jungians consider the habit of dividing the world into fours as an "archetypal" structure genetically passed from parents to children. We could also see this common custom as derived from physical facts. We have mentioned the seasons. Even more basically, the human body gives us four directions: before, behind, right and left.

This last distinction suggests other, more subtle concepts. Beyond the four basic directions, we can also recognize above, below and the center. We have seen in the Major Arcana that these take us to mythological and spiritual levels. Together, these three form the "vertical axis," connecting ourselves in the center to the Light above and the Darkness beneath—the realm of the Gods and land of the dead. The "horizontal axis"—north, south, east and west—signifies the material world. We will encounter the spiritual Above and Below in several Minor cards, especially the Four of Stones. We should also realize that a fifth element exists, connected to the Major Arcana as the fifth suit. We call this "Ether," an invisible essence at one time believed to permeate the universe. Just as the four natural elements represent daily life, so Ether symbolizes spirituality.

Another symbolic system has become joined to the four suits. This is God's four-letter name in Hebrew, YHVH, sometimes called by the Latin name *Tetragrammaton*. The letters are Yod, Heh, Vav, Heh (see Yod in the Hermit, Heh in the Emperor, and Vav in the Hierophant). In Roman letters this becomes YHVH, or IHVH. Since this name appears in the Bible without vowels, we do not know how to pronounce it ("Jehovah" and "Yahweh" are two common approximations). Therefore it has come to signify God's secret and unknowable Name. Religious Jews often refer to God as *HaShem*,

Hebrew for "the Name." This idea of a mystic Word corresponds to the Christian "Logos."

In Jewish folklore this and other secret names took on wondrous powers, so that we read of rabbis performing miracles and flying through the air. The more intellectual Kabbalists have described the Name as a formula of creation. Yod signifies the initial spark. This is the element Fire. The first Heh receives this spark so that a pattern begins to develop. This is Water. We saw in the Major Arcana the fundamental polarity of these two elements and the way creation depends on them joining together. The Vav, by its shape, extends the Yod. It represents Air, or thought, developing the initial pattern. Finally, the last Heh, Earth, becomes the thing created. Notice that the final letter stands apart from the others. The first three describe the process of creation, while the Earth shows the result. P. D. Ouspensky, a mystic psychologist who wrote about the Tarot, put this idea into a diagram.

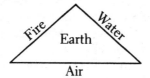

The great model for creation is the Earth. The light of God (Yod) descends into the waters (Heh). God separates (Vav, the shape of a sword) the waters and the firmament, and so creates the world (Heh). We can also apply the same process to any form of human creation as well, from a painting to building a shelf to making dinner. They all proceed from the inspiration to the finished project.

Most of the above applies to the Minor Arcana in general, in the many different Tarot decks. The Haindl Tarot includes one very special feature, the inclusion of a hexagram from the Chinese *I Ching*, or *Book of Changes*, on cards two through ten in each of the suits. Said to be the oldest book in the world, the *I Ching* contains sixty-four hexagrams, each consisting of six lines, either broken or unbroken ( - - or — ). The *I Ching* is an oracle, like the Tarot or the Runes. A person wishing to ask a question throws either three coins or a set of sticks to produce a line. She or he does this six times to get a hexagram. The person then looks up the hexagram in the book and reads the commentary.

Centuries of wisdom have gone into these commentaries. Though the original texts reflect Taoism, Confucius is said to have contributed much of the present interpretations. The *I Ching,* like the Tarot, does not address only the specific situations (though it does that with amazing precision), but also sets the person's question in a wider context, including social conditions, nature, and what we might call "the mood of the cosmos": whether the time favors action or passivity, initiative or patience.

Clearly sixty-four hexagrams will not match thirty-six cards, not in any systematic way. Haindl made his choices subjectively; for each card, he looked through the *I Ching* and chose a hexagram that fit the picture. He used two translations, that of R. L. Wing (a modern version), and the famous poetic version of Richard Wilhelm (rendered in English by Cary F. Baynes). The hexagrams and meanings do not just match the cards. Often they extend what the card has to say. Sometimes they help balance an idea that could become too extreme. The Six of Wands means "Victory," an image Hermann Haindl considers dangerous, for it can imply aggression. Therefore, he gave the card hexagram 2, "The Receptive," the primary image of stillness and devotion.

The use of the *I Ching* for the Minor cards helps give them a wider meaning than that usually found in Tarot decks. Or we might say, it has brought out the wider meanings that already existed. It helps us to see that the particular conditions described in a certain card tell us something about nature and society as well as individual questions. It helps us understand the different needs of different moments. Sometimes, we need to commit ourselves, or take bold action. At other times such action will get us nowhere and we need to wait, or to work behind the scenes. Life is not always the same, and even if two situations appear very similar, the background conditions—or simply the mood of the cosmos—may require very different responses.

Three basic themes in the *I Ching* fit very well with the Haindl Tarot. The first is the idea that extreme conditions create their opposites. The *I Ching* observes this in nature. At the height of summer, we feel the stirrings of autumn. In winter the days get steadily shorter, but then at the darkest point, they turn 'round and begin moving toward spring. In human affairs, the *I Ching* warns us of extreme success, for this can turn over into failure. We see a similar idea in the Haindl Tarot, with the Three of Cups, where great happiness can become too much and spill over into sadness.

The second idea is that of context. Both the *I Ching* and the

Tarot show us four levels (once again, four). These are the individual, society, nature and the cosmos. All of these terms describe physical facts, but they also carry spiritual meanings. More than some Tarot decks, the Haindl Minor Arcana show the way all these levels affect each other.

The third idea, expressed very strongly in these cards, is that of responsibility. If the cosmos can express patterns, it also can express needs. Human beings bear a responsibility to fulfill these needs, to enable nature to heal itself, and spiritual truth to become realized in the physical world.

The idea of God as incomplete, of human beings as agents of God's evolution, is fundamental to occult philosophy. It deeply informs the Major Arcana of the Tarot and in this deck, the numbered cards of the Minor Arcana as well. (In the Court cards we see it more subtly as the Native American idea of all creatures helping the Creator.) One of the greatest of Kabbalists, Isaac Luria, described God's light as scattered, buried in the broken pieces of the Tree of Life. It becomes each person's responsibility to liberate the light and return it to itself. In the Haindl Tarot we see a similar idea in regard to the Earth. Human recklessness and greed have wounded nature. The responsibility is ours to restore it.

As with the Major cards I have given particular divinatory meanings for each of these cards in readings. However, we should not consider these meanings as something apart from the main description. In the tradition of the Minor Arcana, the entire commentary for each card belongs to the card's interpretation. To use these cards for readings, therefore, consider what the description *and* the specific suggestions say, in the light of the other cards and the person's question.

# THE SUIT OF WANDS

THE SUIT OF Wands symbolizes the element Fire. Fire is energetic, courageous, dynamic. It symbolizes movement, excitement, creative energy. As the first letter in God's name it signifies beginnings. Fire takes the initiative. It desires to begin new projects or try out new ideas. By itself, this energy may not follow through on its grand beginnings. Just as flames flicker, so this kind of approach to life looks for constant change. And remember that the hottest flames burn out the quickest. Pure fire needs constant fuel, constant excitement and newness.

Fire symbolizes the divine spark, the mystery of life, which makes a human being more than a machine. In the Major Arcana we described this energy as the Shakti, and we referred to the image of Shiva lying inert as stone without that sacred Fire. (In the Court cards we will see this idea from the other side, with Kali taking the energy back from a dead Shiva.) We saw as well how when people awaken the energy in the body, they experience great heat.

The Greek myth of Prometheus tells how he stole Fire from the Gods and gave it to humanity. Modern interpretations of this story tend to see this Fire as a metaphor for technology. And indeed Fire signifies the ability of humans to make new things out of raw nature. But the myth states that Prometheus stole *divine* Fire, that which gives the Gods their immortality. Zeus had wanted to destroy humans, but when Prometheus gave them the spark of true life, destruction became impossible.

The symbol for Wands in this deck is the spear (also called a lance). Spears are weapons, but not necessarily symbols of human conflict, for they probably originated in hunting rather than warfare. Hunting symbolizes masculine power. Though we usually think of Fire and Wands as individualistic (as in the Magician, who in most Tarot decks holds a magic wand), hunting implies harmony, for the tribe has more success when the men hunt together. Hunting develops an intimate and sacred relationship with nature. The hunters pray to the animals, asking for help and begging forgiveness for taking their lives. This bond becomes so powerful in some societies

10

that the hunters take on part of the qualities of the main animals they hunt.

In the early Grail mysteries, the spear probably symbolized the masculine solar energy awaking life in the womb and the Earth. We saw this idea with the spear and cup in the card of the Lovers. The Christian version changed this emphasis, bringing in the idea of aggression and misuse of power. Here the spear does become a weapon, the very lance used to wound Christ on the cross. When the Grail came to England (see the Ace of Cups) so did the spear. In some versions of the story, a knight finds himself chased through the Grail castle by an enemy. He enters a room where he sees a sleeping (or wounded) king, and a spear dripping blood. Ignoring the sacred power in the room he grabs the spear and strikes his enemy. This "dolorous stroke" destroys the castle and all the land around it, for he has taken the holy power and used it for personal advantage.

The allegory describes a problem with Wands, that of arrogance, insensitivity and misuse of power. It comes from the great confidence that Fire brings, the feeling you can burn up whatever stands in your way. And yet, as we saw above, fire can burn itself out. A great start, great ideas and plans, will come to nothing without the ability to develop them. The bursting energy of the Nine of Wands can change to the failure of the Ten of Wands. Therefore, we need to use the Wands' energy when we have it, and we need to use it wisely. Unfortunately, the nature of Fire makes us believe it will last forever. By reminding us of the other elements, the Tarot helps us to balance Fire with such qualities as sensitivity and steadiness.

# THE ACE OF WANDS

The Aces link the numbered cards to the Court cards of the same suit. While the other numbered cards, two through ten, show various states, or moments, in the changing patterns of life, the Aces belong to the same cultural and spiritual traditions as the Court cards. They show the tradition in its most basic expression. Thus we see in this picture the "lingam and yoni," the phallic stone and the pool of water, the male and female aspects of God mixed together. The lingam—the stone—represents Shiva, while the yoni symbolizes Shakti/Parvati/Kali (the three primary names of the Goddess).

Ace of Wands in the East

They are the two poles of existence, the fundamental energies, and their union allows the creation and sustenance of the universe.

When Hermann Haindl traveled in India he visited the area around the town of Bhinarvan, the birthplace of Krishna and Radha (see the Son and Daughter of Wands). When he took walks in the forest he would sometimes find an old tree marked with orange. The orange symbolized Fire, and marked the spot as sacred. At the base of the tree would be a small lingam and yoni, placed there as a shrine. In that land of complex art and elaborate decoration, these shrines to the God and Goddess formed the simplest temples.

Phallic stones are found in many places besides India. We see them, for instance, in the Celtic lands of Western Europe, especially Brittany. In some places phallic stones guard crossroads, for the cross, too, symbolizes a joining of energies. The Vatican contains an ancient phallic stone, from the days when it served as an archaic temple, and later a temple to Mithras, before Christianity became the state religion.

In the picture the lingam appears a deep red, almost purple. This suggests sexual arousal, but we should not assume that the lingam only means male sexuality. Masculine lust and energy are seen as one expression of the creative force of the God, that which gives life, which brings the light of the Sun, the seed that awakens the egg in the womb. Flames surround the top of the stone and the top of the spear. These do signify lust and sexual energy. To understand this card—and the Tarot in general—we need to overcome the conditioning that makes us see sex as the opposite of spirituality. But the flames also signify the immortal spark which makes each of us more than just our physical forms.

While the lingam shows only red, all colors appear in the yoni. This indicates the potentiality of the female principle. All things remain possible in the state symbolized by Water. Fire is active. It moves and carries energy. A spear heads in one direction. The yoni symbolizes stillness and receptivity. In the state before action, all choices remain open (compare also the Magician and the High Priestess).

In connection with Court cards, the Aces represent archaic symbols. In connection with the other numbers they represent the basic element of the card. They signify that element as the "root" of the various experiences shown in the cards two through ten. The Ace of Wands, therefore, signifies Fire, creative force, beginnings, desire, movement.

We see, in fact, all the elements in this card. Water appears as the yoni, but also in the background, behind the grass. We see dirt and plants representing Earth, and the sky for Air. The plants take the same form as the flame. This shows us that living creatures, plants as well as animals, depend on Fire, for plants cannot grow without the Sun. We can describe plants as a fixed form of Fire. The Water, however, remains completely itself, for Water is the counterpart of fire.

## DIVINATORY MEANINGS

In readings, the card signifies the "gift" of Fire in a person's life. It is a time of energy, of optimism and confidence. These qualities may express themselves in work, or in relationships, or in creativity. If the reading refers to sexuality, the Ace of Wands indicates desire and great sexual energy. It may be necessary to balance this with the kind of emotional commitment and sensitivity shown in such cards as the Two of Cups.

The Ace of Wands is a card of beginnings. It indicates inspiration, an auspicious start for projects, a new job, moving to a new house. The card symbolizes courage, but also self-indulgence.

## REVERSED

The reversed Ace of Wands shows that the person finds it hard to focus his or her energy. Efforts become scattered or confused, and situations around the person may seem chaotic or lacking in harmony. The person may find it difficult to move events in a desired way. The card may indicate pessimism or a loss of self-confidence. In a more positive sense, and in connection with such cards as the High Priestess or the Hermit, the Ace of Wands reversed suggests that this is not the time for action. The person needs to seek quiet and not try to initiate new projects.

## TWO OF WANDS—DOMINION

The name of this card suggests power and control. The setting of a ruined church, however, indicates that it does not concern personal or political power so much as the power of the soul. Because it shows an old church it implies that sacred power has been neglected in our time. Nevertheless, it still exists, like a hidden force within our world.

The image of a church takes the sacred Fire of the Ace and gives it a form. This is indeed the ideal of a Church as an institution—that it give shape and meaning to the mystical experiences that inspire religion. As official religions become more political, more concerned with power in the narrow sense, their buildings may become grander but the true Church will have decayed from neglect. And so in this picture we see an ancient building, one that has fallen down in parts, but which keeps its original meaning.

Dominion
Two of Wands

The *I Ching* hexagram is 26, called by Wing "Potential Energy" and by Wilhelm the wonderful title, "The Taming Power of the Great." Both emphasize the need to hold firm to correct action, to follow through on something. Wilhelm stresses learning from the wisdom of the past, a theme we see in the ancient building. Wing says this is a time to begin new and ambitious projects. Creative energy runs through the hexagram. This tells us that the power described in the card's title does not exist somewhere beyond us, but in ourselves.

The picture here comes from a painting titled *Kathedrale*, done in 1983 after Haindl visited Saint Anne's in Jerusalem. We see in the center a broken-down staircase, one used again and again for different temples built on the same site. A staircase symbolizes a spiritual ascent, the soul rising to heaven. The stairs lead up to a place where the roof has broken open to reveal the sky. The church is not just a human construction. And as we saw with the Ace (and the Hanged Man), the earliest temples were special places in nature.

The front of the picture is light, the back dark, signifying the mystery at the center of any religion. The outer teachings may sound very clear but the inner truth remains hidden until we follow the kind of path depicted in the Major Arcana.

The columns of the church rise up like lingams. The arches, however, form yonis. Again we learn the lesson that existence depends on both kinds of energy. The two forms merge one into the other.

The two spears form what is called a Saint Andrew's cross. They also form the gift Rune from the card of the Sun. We also see the Rune Mann, the posture of a person with arms crossed over the chest. This gesture is a powerful one. Haindl has seen it as the gesture of Osiris in ancient paintings. He has also seen it as an Arabic greeting, done with the phrase *Salaam Alaykam,* "Peace be with you." We make this peaceful gesture with the hands open and the palms flat against the body, an indication of no weaponry (holding out the right hand carries the same meaning in Europe). But if we stand upright with arms crossed over the chest and fists closed, it produces a circuit of powerful energy in the body. (This is still not aggressive, for the energy is not directed outward. In fact, the inward quality is what produces the power.) In a meditation using postures for each of the first seven trump cards, I have found that this latter gesture works well with the Chariot. As a symbol of power, we often find two crossed lances on a coat of arms.

When we look at the spears themselves we see power. If we look at the way they divide spaces, we see that the two spears form four quadrants. Traditionally the number four signifies law, both cosmic and human. Power needs to follow the inner patterns of life to produce a worthwhile effect. If we go against these patterns our strength becomes destructive or simply lost. We might also add that society's laws need to follow these patterns or they become corrupt.

In modern road signs X means "do not enter." Hermann Haindl has said that he did not mean the spears to block the church. His wife, Erica Haindl, has pointed out that the inner mysteries do not stand open to everyone. We need to find our own way inside.

## DIVINATORY MEANINGS

In readings, this card speaks of power, of someone established and successful. He or she has a strong position in life as well as personal strength of will. There is a need to use this power wisely and in line with deeper principles rather than personal advantage or control of others. In line with the hexagram, it may indicate a choice to build power, that is, to begin ambitious projects. In its deepest sense, the card indicates discovering the power of spiritual truth.

## REVERSED

The reversed Two of Wands shows a person voluntarily giving up a position of power. The person may wish to find a new direction, or to seek adventures by traveling. In questions about work it can mean looking for a new job or a whole new career. Another interpretation of the reversed card would suggest a misuse of power.

## THREE OF WANDS—VIRTUE

The background for the Three of Wands comes from the same painting as the previous one. Again we see the broken-down cathedral, here with a window open to the sky. The building remains, signifying humanity's ancient need to give structure to religious feeling. However, the stained glass that once might have filled such a window has vanished. The complex theologies and philosophies have broken down. What remains is true virtue, in which people act in a holy way from an awareness of truth.

The hexagram is 50. Wing calls it "Cosmic Order" and describes it as great good fortune. Such fortune comes, he says, when human needs lie in harmony with the needs (patterns) of the cosmos. This idea hints that in the view of the *I Ching* (or the Tarot), change in nature does not occur randomly, however it might appear to our limited perception. Instead, it fulfills the needs of the cosmos, following an order too vast for us to comprehend. A book of changes, then, does not tell us simply how to get rich and avoid quarrels. It helps us align ourselves with the needs of the cosmos.

Virtue
Three of Wands

Wilhelm also describes this hexagram as "supreme good fortune." He titles it "Cauldron" because the shape of the lines suggests a pot with a lid, resting on two short legs. The Cauldron and
the Well (hexagram 48, the Ten of Stones), represent the only two
human-made objects to appear as hexagram images. This brings us
back to the theme of culture.

The third spear changes the Rune from Gebo to Hagall, the
Mother of Runes, a link to the Empress, the Chariot, and various
others. Hagall brings balance, and harmony with the patterns of life.
The truly virtuous person acts from a sense of fulfilling his or her
own purpose, of helping the world to achieve its goals. Occult doctrine teaches that we do not come into the world just to obey blindly
a set of laws and then receive judgment after death. Rather, God
and the universe are themselves evolving and we form part of the

instruments of that evolution. By acting in harmony with an individual purpose in life a person helps fulfill the needs of the cosmos.

When Hermann and Erica Haindl and I discussed this card, we considered the implications of the crumbling church. Erica said it takes us back before the official Church. Hermann pointed out that we no longer can imagine what it was like when religion was new and fresh.

## DIVINATORY MEANINGS

In readings this card can carry a great significance. It can indicate that the person acts in harmony with nature and with the needs of the situation. If the person wants to know "Am I doing the right thing?" the Three of Wands answers yes. More generally, it can show that the person has found his or her purpose in life and can go ahead with confidence. The hexagram implies that good fortune will result. However, the other cards may indicate opposition.

## REVERSED

The reversed Three of Wands shows a person out of harmony with the situation. He or she may be struggling to find the best course of action. The reversed card may show someone who finds it hard to see a point to life, or discover goals that seem truly worthwhile.

# FOUR OF WANDS—PERFECTION

The Four of Wands also comes from *Kathedrale* (as does the Nine of Wands). When we look at the card we see the bubble with the eye in the middle. When we look closer we see that the bubble rests in a hand coming down from above as if presenting a gift.

The hexagram is 63, called "After Completion" by Wilhelm and "After the End" by Wing. This describes a situation in which peace and harmony have been achieved. Chaos has given way to order and there is a sense of perfection. Wilhelm says that the strong and weak

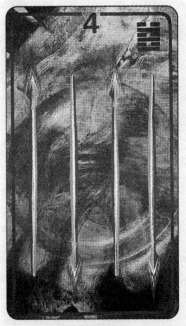

Perfection
Four of Wands

lines occupy the right places. However, in the Chinese view, one state changes into another. Therefore, if we reach an apex—a perfect moment—we can easily fall. In the midst of perfection we need caution and persistence, for small mistakes at such a time can bring large changes.

In most of the Wands cards, the spears all point up. This belongs to the idea of Fire, which in nature leaps upward. Fire represents optimism and eagerness. It shows a desire to climb to higher levels. But such an emphasis on rising creates an imbalance, for as we have seen with the spiral symbols in the Major Arcana, spirituality does not simply ascend away from the world, but returns into it. The divine Fire comes "down" to us as a gift. In this picture we not only see the hand descending to give us the ball, but we also find two spears pointing down alternately with the two pointing up. This shows that "Perfection" depends on a balance of energies.

We have described the number four as symbolizing law. Here we see 4 as 2 x 2, a reminder that laws and structures need to carry within them the inner truth symbolized by the High Priestess. The pattern of spears also suggests the famous maxim, "As above, so below." This phrase means that the various forms and patterns of ordinary life mirror the cosmic patterns of divine law. The expression carries a special meaning for divination. Astrologers interpret it literally. The patterns of individual lives ("below") reflect, or derive from, the patterns of the stars and planets ("above"). In other forms of divination, the phrases indicate that the mix of Tarot cards, or the fall of sticks for the *I Ching,* carry meaning because they reflect the meaningful patterns of a person's life. And further—the idea we saw in the last card—that life itself carries meaning because it reflects cosmic order and purpose.

"Above" and "below" also mean heaven and the underworld, the mythological realms of light and darkness. As we saw in the Major Arcana, we need to explore both these realms in ourselves in order to reach the liberation shown in the triumphs. One of the world's oldest poems, the Sumerian epic "The Descent of Inanna," describes how the Queen of Heaven goes to her sister, the Goddess of Death. It begins, "From the Great Above she turned her ear to the Great Below."

In the painting *Kathedrale* a tree grows in the center of the broken church. The trunk of the tree appears like stone. New life grows from the ruins of the old. The bubble, too, indicates new possibilities. We have seen, in such cards as the Empress, the High Priestess and Aeon, the importance of this image in the Haindl Tarot. The eye, too, reminds us of Aeon, with the ancient eye looking out from behind the clouds. This eye has not quite opened, not quite emerged from the stone.

Though the hand coming down signifies a gift, it also recalls the hand in the Wheel of Fortune. That image symbolizes the need to take our fate in our hands. Here we should realize that if a hand reaches out to us with a gift, we need to extend our own hand in order to take it. If life gives us new opportunities, we need to act in order to take advantage of them.

## DIVINATORY MEANINGS

For readings, the meanings of the Four of Wands include the idea of new life, new possibilities. The card tells us to look out for opportunities, and to make sure we take action at the right moment. More broadly, it signifies a feeling of renewal in a person's life. This is a feeling of excitement, of growth. If action is necessary, so is humility. The powerful Fire energy can lead to arrogance. The spears pointing down remind the person to keep a sense of balance. Otherwise, the possibilities can be lost.

## REVERSED

Reversed, the Four of Wands can indicate errors or going in the wrong direction. The person may be too eager for a new beginning. It may be necessary to wait for a genuine opportunity.

# FIVE OF WANDS—CONFLICT

As the title implies, this is one of the more difficult cards in the suit of Wands. The idea of conflict actually belongs to Fire, because the aggressive energy seeks to test itself in battle. This can lead to positive results, when the people involved see the battle as a thrilling game. We speak of such things as "the conflict of ideas" or "creative struggle." But when one side seeks dominance at all costs—rather than the creative release of its own energy—then the conflict turns into something much harsher than a game.

The hexagram, 49, means "Revolution" in Wilhelm and "Changing" in Wing. In modern times we tend to look favorably on revolution. The French, the Americans, the Russians, the Chinese, and so on, all celebrate their own revolutions. When a new revolution happens, people outside treat the new group positively, at least until they do things the outside world dislikes. In other situations, such as science or the arts, "revolution" means a dynamic change, bringing great improvements and opportunities. The I Ching, however, values stability and harmony. It seeks smooth, gradual change rather than violent reversals. Therefore, hexagram 49 implies danger, chaos, extreme situations. Revolution should only hap-

Conflict
Five of Wands

pen when the situation has gotten so out of balance that no gentle approach will work. Part of the purpose of the *I Ching* is to prevent such dangers from arising by showing people how to act in harmony with the moment.

The picture in the Five of Wands shows a detail from a Haindl painting named *Oedipus*. We see the top of a stone column—another lingam. The column appears to be changing shape, merging into the organic, like the stone tree in *Kathedrale*. This theme of transformation belongs with Fire, which changes things from one form to another, melting solids, turning liquids into gas. The top of the column resembles the brain in shape. This links the column with the spine so that the picture suggests the human body.

At the same time the column is dark and chaotic, symbolizing, among other possibilities, the violence of history. The Haindls and I discussed this card at their house in Italy, near the city of Pisa.

Erica remarked that Pisa once possessed two red columns, symbols of Christ (again, the lingam for the male principle). When Florence conquered Pisa it stole the columns, thereby taking the people's spiritual center.

The spears rise up from the dark below, as if striving to go away from the dark bloody past. But as we saw in the Devil and the Tower, we need to come to terms, not only with history, but with our own inner darkness. Conflict often comes from people projecting their own fears and anger outward onto enemies.

The spears do not rise equally, but with one higher than the others. This symbolizes hierarchy, which Hermann Haindl sees as a source of conflict and aggression. The idea of one person or class considered superior to another leads to war and slavery. It also leads to the subjugation of women by men who justify this with claims of male superiority and divine law.

The spears also symbolize the intellect's desire to leave the Earth, or to conquer nature as a means of escaping our origins as animals. Intellectual energy can represent the positive side of this card. For example, the decoding of DNA came partly through competition among scientists; with this knowledge doctors can seek better ways to treat genetic diseases. At the same time intellectual striving can lead to a break with reality, as when people see the making of terrible weapons as an interesting puzzle.

## DIVINATORY MEANINGS

When the Five of Wands appears in readings right side up, we tend to look at its more positive aspects. It shows energy, excitement, people striving and battling but without hatred or bitterness. We can think of the person having thrown the spears, like a hunter seeking prey. The Five of Wands can be a card of someone active in the world. Still, we should not forget the dark chaos at the bottom. There may be areas of the person's life he or she wants to avoid or escape. The other cards will indicate whether this presents a problem.

## REVERSED

The Five of Wands reversed emphasizes the more unhappy aspects. The conflicts become stronger, more personal and aggressive. Notice that when we reverse the card the spears come back at us, as if thrown by others. The reversed card sometimes indicates bitterness at other people's behavior.

## SIX OF WANDS—VICTORY

After the battle of Five comes the Victory. The Six of Wands is a very positive card, showing the Wands' qualities of power and triumph. For Hermann Haindl, however, Victory can be as difficult a subject as Conflict, for the idea of a winner can imply someone else losing. Therefore, he has used the hexagram and the background to balance the Wands' aggression. There are also different ways to interpret the theme of Victory. It can signify a personal victory over one's own doubts or handicaps. It can indicate the kind of triumph where a group of people work together to achieve something important. The six spears stand all at the same height, suggesting cooperation. We can also see them as no longer rising but having reached a high level—together.

The hexagram is 2, "The Receptive" in Wilhelm, "Natural Response" in Wing. One of the two primary hexagrams, it consists of six yin lines. If we turn the card on its side we see that the spears form six yang lines. This is hexagram 1, "The Creative," seen on the Two of Cups. The card, therefore, contains both hexagrams, each balancing the other. The main attribute of the Receptive is devotion. The person enacts the moment by following rather than leading. The hexagram also embodies the Earth, and darkness, just as the Creative embodies the Sky and light. Fire, Wands, belongs to the light. And Fire leaps up toward heaven. Hexagram 2, therefore, balances the card.

The background shows a detail from a picture called "Dionysus." The very subject of the picture helps to balance, or transcend, the personal victory. Dionysus was a god of ecstasy, leading his followers in the ancient dance. Hermann Haindl sees this as prerational, before intellectual definitions of the world. Ecstasy represents a collective victory, over isolation, over limited perceptions of

Victory
Six of Wands

reality, over death, for in ecstasy we gain a sense of eternity beyond the body.

The brown lines at the bottom are Dionysus's hair. In the card we see them more as the brown Earth, with vines of ivy growing. Haindl painted the ivy thinking of his home in Italy. The plant also signifies victory, for in northern Europe people made wreaths from ivy, just as the Romans used laurel. Ivy remains green in winter, the time when the land lies dead; the plant signifies triumph over death. This, too, represents a victory without victims.

## DIVINATORY MEANINGS

In readings the Six of Wands indicates triumph, but also the confidence and firm action that will lead to triumph. It indicates great optimism and belief, often inspiring others. The person may need to watch out that others do not suffer because of his or her victory. If the other cards indicate such a problem, the person may wish to look for ways to cooperate rather than compete. In its best sense the Six of Wands shows a person who can inspire others with belief and confidence in ultimate success. This card and the card of the Universe together in a reading would give a positive sign to any undertaking.

## REVERSED

The Six of Wands reversed shows a loss of belief. It does not indicate failure so much as a negative attitude that can lead to failure. It speaks of self-doubt, hesitation. The person needs to realize that both defeat and victory can come out of self-fulfilling prophecies.

## SEVEN OF WANDS—COURAGE

Like the last card, the Seven of Wands also represents something of a problem, to Hermann Haindl. The idea of Courage suggests war, when officers demand that soldiers show courage to kill or to die, whichever comes first. As with the previous card, we can find other meanings for courage, including even pacifism. The trump of the Chariot indicates great courage to deal with the mysteries and terrors of one's own existence. In thinking about this whole series of cards we need to remember Haindl's own experiences as a young man in the war, and then the years afterward, when Germany had to face a destroyed nation as well as the horror of discovering what had happened in the camps.

The hexagram is 40, titled "Liberation" by Wing and "Deliverance" by Wilhelm. It calls for firm action to overcome anxiety in the self and conflict with others. The commentary for the hexagram cites the image of a thunderstorm clearing the air on a hot day. The image stresses relief rather than conquest. The purpose of courage is not to subdue others, but to remove problems. The image of a thunderstorm can also suggest the pair of the Tower and the Star. There the explosion brings renewal and a new openness.

The picture shows a scene of rocks at sea. The scene is peaceful, though the sky appears gray with clouds, indicating a possible

Courage
Seven of Wands

storm. Courage at sea is different than courage in battle; in a storm at sea the sailors must all work together to survive.

The spears rise out of holes in the rock, like lingams rising from yonis. The spear symbolizes active humanity striving upward. The rock symbolizes nature and our eternal ties to the Earth. The rocks appear vaguely like stone faces, or statues, so old they have lost all detail. If we place this card beside the Ten of Cups, from the same painting, we will see them as two faces looking at each other.

The bottom half of a ball appears in the top part of the Seven of Wands. This recalls the Universe, with the rocks here taking on the shape of the dragon. Remember that the mythological serpent lay coiled at the bottom of the sea. This image hints at a deeper kind of courage, to uncoil the dragon and seek transformation.

In the Universe the ball was the Earth. Here it signifies the non-material world of the mystic. The spears rise out of the rock toward heaven, as if striving to reach the ball. If we see the movement as a desire to escape the Earth it will fail, for the Earth forms the basis of our reality. But we can look at the movement as the courage to transform aggression into something deeper.

## DIVINATORY MEANINGS

In readings the Seven of Wands emphasizes its fundamental attribute—it shows a person with courage and daring. The way he or she uses the courage can become a vital issue. Is it for conquest or personal development? Does it lead to something important, or just a love of battle? All situations call for courage. Sometimes we need to recognize weakness, or limitations, or an impossible situation that cannot be saved. Courage may mean the courage to retreat. In its deepest sense this card means having the courage to use one's own power for transformation.

## REVERSED

The Seven of Wands reversed shows, first of all, a loss of nerve. The person hesitates, finds it hard to continue. Such a meaning would become emphasized with the Chariot reversed, or similar cards. But the reversed Seven of Wands may also serve as advice. Avoid the path of courage. Seek an alternative—possibly reconciliation.

# EIGHT OF WANDS—SWIFTNESS

The title of this card implies movement, progress in different directions. Since the spears move upward, they indicate that the movement includes spiritual development. This may include a movement from confusion to clarity, weakness to strength, doubt to belief.

The hexagram for the Eight of Wands is 35, "Progress" in both Wing and Wilhelm. This idea, too, relates to movement, especially this image of movement upward. As a book rooted in ancient China, the *I Ching* sometimes includes metaphors that strike us as quaint.

Swiftness
Eight of Wands

For Progress the book says, "The prince is honored with horses. In a single day he is granted audience three times." The modern explanation by Wing stresses that a person makes progress when he or she fulfills the needs of society. Individual ambition serves a greater purpose and so gains energy from being part of the pattern.

Wilhelm says that the nature of man is good but may need perfecting. He compares this to sunlight. Light itself is pure, but sometimes becomes obscured by mists rising from the Earth. When it rises high in the sky the sun burns off the fog. Again we find the same image as in the card, the rising upward. The spears join a dark lower-right corner to a bright area in the upper left.

We also see red, as of fire, or blood, in the lower-left corner. This gives way to blue, the Sky. The impulse for movement comes from the fiery life energy, which desires action. But that swift movement carries us to a purer level. We might recall that the Sky and the earth are not just intellectual symbols. In ecstatic states, or even simply in natural settings, we experience the Earth and Sky in very different ways. To root ourselves in the Earth (none of the Spears leave the rock), but then allow consciousness to rise to the blue sky, gives a sense of liberation.

The spears appear all in a straight line. When we look closer we see that this is an illusion. The card does not show an abstract principle, but an experience. The spears move from back to front. This, too, gives a positive quality to Swiftness. People come forward, they emerge from the shadows into the light. This card can symbolize the development of a strong personality.

The open space combines the lingam and yoni. Like the arch of the cathedral it shows a hole, like the womb. But the shape of that hole resembles the phallic column.

The spears all move in the same direction. Swiftness comes when all energy focuses on a single goal. The movement, however, is not aggressive. The spears follow the Empress/Hanged Man direction, rooted on the left—the side of peace, and moving to the right—the side of action. The movement up shows confidence. When we discussed this card, Haindl told me of the symbol for the S.P.D. in the Weimar Republic, ✓✓✓. The downward direction gave a negative quality. The Republic fell to the aggressive energy of the Nazis. (The Nazis themselves expressed a violent nihilism in their symbol. Their version of the swastika, which they took from the image of Thor's hammer, rotates counterclockwise, the direction of dissolution.)

The spears cross a diagonal line made by the rock. This forms eight X's, or gift Runes. Swiftness is a gift in life, for it can only happen when all our own efforts and the situation around us line up together, in the way the spears line up. The crossing lines also hint at the Rune Othal, which united the yang and yin energies.

## DIVINATORY MEANINGS

In readings, the Eight of Wands indicates definite movement, often toward particular goals. It shows progress, hints at success, and suggests that the goal is a worthy one. It can indicate a person finding a direction in life, or a purpose. Meditating with this card can help to focus energy, to bring various scattered activities into line with each other. The rootedness of the spears reminds us that we should not forget basic values as we move toward our goals. In romantic situations, the card can mean the development of a new love affair.

## REVERSED

The Eight of Wands reversed shows that the energy is more scattered. The person finds it difficult to focus on a goal, and so wastes time and effort with contradictory activities. It can indicate negativism, especially with similar cards, such as the Six of Wands reversed. The card can mean hesitation, the fear of taking action. In regard to love, it suggests shyness, or sometimes jealousy.

## NINE OF WANDS—POWER

With the Nine of Wands we return to *Kathedrale*. The use of this painting four times in the Wands gives the suit a more spiritual quality than it carries in most Tarot decks. This is fitting, since the Haindl Tarot is a spiritual work, dealing with the joys and problems of sacred reality. The spears thrust upward and out, an image of bursting energy. As well as the spears, the phallic tree gives a sense of masculine energy. However, the tree also symbolizes the power of nature.

The ideal of male power moves from the sexual image to the military in the hexagram, number 7, called by Wilhelm, "The Army" and by Wing, "Collective Force." The *I Ching* examines this institution and its purposes. The commentary considers military action a last resort. The army, it says, must work toward a clear goal, with the support of the people. In a wider sense this implies the idea that power must have a purpose. In political situations, a strong army often leads to oppression of neighbors, simply because the temptation exists to use the army. In many societies the army becomes an extension of male virility. On the personal level, power can carry the same danger, the desire to use it simply because one has it.

Wing gives the hexagram a more general interpretation. The power of the group, he says, requires discipline and organization, but also righteous aims. Again we find the problem of power wanting to exercise itself, a sense we get from the image here of the

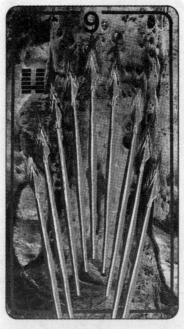

Power
Nine of Wands

spears pushing out as well as up. Like sexuality, power desires objects. It yearns to express itself. A person receiving this card in a
reading should recognize his or her power but also make sure the
energy finds a worthy outlet.

We described, in the Four of Wands, how a tree grows from the
center of the cathedral. Here we see the base of the tree. The trunk
merges wood and stone, with no clear sense of which is which. Eyes
appear in the upper trunk, the eyes of birds. In the archaic magical
view of life, anything can change into anything else.

At this time in the world the power of human culture appears
ascendant over nature, with forests vanishing and rivers dying.
Some scientists theorize that this process exists independently of
human desire, and will eventually replace nature entirely, with bio-
engineering providing oxygen, food and water. Before we accept
this fate we might think of the once-great cities covered by jungle

in such places as the Yucatan. Or, more simply, the way plants will break through the concrete of a New York sidewalk. If humans somehow vanished from Manhattan Island, how long would it take for the forest to reclaim the land? This, then, is another kind of power, that of life to assert itself, over and over, against all attempts to control or crush it.

Hermann Haindl comments that the oval space to the left of the tree resembles the vulva. But this yoni has become detached from the lingam (compare the Ace), a sign of the danger when the thrusting yang energy loses the counterbalance of yin stillness and receptivity.

## DIVINATORY MEANINGS

In readings the Nine of Wands indicates great energy in the person, the feeling that you can overpower the whole world. As mentioned above, the person needs to find a worthwhile object for this power. Otherwise it can lead to dominating weaker people. The person should also recognize that not everyone shares this sense of power. Because Wands energy looks at life so optimistically, it can lead to arrogance, especially toward those who feel weak.

In readings dealing with sex, the card shows great sexual energy. Since this energy alone does not guarantee successful relationships (or even a relationship at all—desire becomes a problem when it cannot find an outlet), the reader will need to look at the other cards to see where this energy leads.

The card can also represent life's resiliency. A person who has suffered great sorrow, or oppression, will come back with renewed energy. This card would come as a good omen in a reading that otherwise shows pain or weakness.

## REVERSED

The Nine of Wands reversed shows the person feeling weak or passive. This is not necessarily a bad thing, if the situation calls for quietness or patience. The positive qualities of this card, when reversed, would become emphasized with such cards as the High Priestess or the Hermit.

The reversed Nine of Wands can also stress the more difficult sides of the crowd, the arrogance or misuse of power.

## TEN OF WANDS—OPPRESSION

This card is a kind of mirror of the previous one, the Nine of Wands—Power. That card showed great power to abuse as well as to help. With the Ten of Wands, the person becomes the victim of such power. In cards six through nine, the spears all point upward, symbol of confidence. This movement reaches its limit in card 9. As we saw in the introduction, Wands power, by its nature, assumes it will last forever. But a Book of Changes, the Tarot as well as the *I Ching*, teaches that going completely in one direction is dangerous, for life can flip over to the other side. As unbalanced as the 9, the 10 card shows all the spears pointing downward. The background comes from a painting of cats hunting mice. But in this fragment the situation has turned round. A flying mouse—a bat—swoops down on frightened cats.

The hexagram is 54, called by Wilhelm, "The Marrying Maiden" and by Wing, "Subordinate." In the Chinese social order, a man usually took a second wife. This woman had to remain passive, for her place gave her little power in the household. Wing modernizes the hexagram and describes it as a situation where you depend completely on others who depend not at all on you. In this situation you cannot take the initiative (a basic Wands quality), for without power, bold actions will fail.

The problem comes partly from situations defined only in terms of place and influence. If people arrange their relationships by affection rather than power they can avoid such victor/victim conditions. But Wands energy seeks conquest. When we come out on top it seems desirable and natural. We forget the other side until it happens to us, until the cats find themselves hunted by the bat. This is an unnatural state for the hunters. The cats cower, with no ground seen underneath them. They are lost and confused.

However, the message is not entirely bleak, as it first appears. The dark at the bottom changes to white at the top. When we look again at the bat we see feathers on the wings, as if the bat transforms into a bird. Since birds and whiteness symbolize spirituality we see oppression giving way to wisdom. If Wands represent arrogance,

Oppression
Ten of Wands

then sometimes we need to experience the other side in order to become more caring. The bird equivalent of a bat is an owl. Both hunt
and both fly at night. We know from the Hermit that an owl symbolizes wisdom and dreams. The world of the spirits lifts us beyond
conditions based only on influence and subordination.

## DIVINATORY MEANINGS

In readings, the Ten of Wands refers to its title—oppressive situations. The person may feel weak or inferior, without power to
bring changes. The other cards may show that this view exaggerates
the actual problems. The card can indicate depression, when a person feels helpless. The reader needs to point out that the card shows
a transformation from dark to light, cruelty to liberation. If the other

cards show a person going from one success to another, with a danger of arrogance, the Ten of Wands can serve as a warning of a possible fall. The person may need to pay more attention to details, or to other people's feelings.

## REVERSED

When we reverse the card of oppression, the Ten of Wands, it shows the person emerging from a bad situation. A change is coming in the external conditions, or the person has refused to accept the position of victim. The hexagram reminds us that one cannot always make such a change, just by willing it or taking action. If conditions do not present success, then action may bring more trouble. It may be necessary to wait. Still, reversing the card of oppression usually shows a positive change.

The image of the bat metamorphosing into an owl suggests wisdom gained from a bad situation. The reversed Ten of Wands would emphasize this aspect of the card. It would also imply that such wisdom leads to liberation. This becomes especially true when we take the card to mean depression.

# THE SUIT OF CUPS

CUPS IS THE suit of Water. Of the four Grail symbols the Cup is the Grail itself, an image we will also explore in the Ace. Water is shapeless, constantly changing; therefore, it represents feeling, which is not rigid or solid, but always shifting. We each pass through many emotional states in a single day, even a single hour; our moods change so subtly and quickly we usually do not notice all the variations.

While water signifies all emotional states, the suit of Cups emphasizes joyous experiences: love, dreams, desire, happiness. Sorrow and conflict appear more in Swords.

Cups and Water belong to the yin, or female, pole. Traditionally, love and happiness are seen as feminine concerns. Books and films for women deal with romance and family, while those for men concern struggle and achievement. By showing these qualities in different suits, neither of which is considered superior to the others, the Tarot shows that all are necessary. The idea of happiness as female can be traced back to the Great Mother's love for her children. In many societies men go out to hunt or make war, while women care for the crops and the children.

Sexual love, too, is shown as female, in the figure of Aphrodite/ Venus, Goddess of love. Love is different than lust, which means desire without emotional involvement. If we think of pure physical desire as Wands, then Cups completes the Fire suit, by adding feeling to arousal. Love as feminine also derives from the "courtly love" tradition of the Middle Ages, in which the knight revered the lady as a kind of goddess. In her service he would attempt great acts of courage. The later versions of the Grail stories became linked to this tradition when they were attached to the King Arthur legends.

We should recognize that the cup and the water are not the same. The cup holds the water, contains it in a form. This evokes the idea of giving some form and understanding to shapeless emotions. In the Major Arcana we saw Water as mystery, the sea as the unconscious. In the Minor Arcana, Water is given a more recognizable meaning; that is, the cards here deal with the daily experiences of our feelings.

A cup is something created by culture. A cup is meant to be used. At the same time it does not have to do anything. It fulfills its purpose simply by receiving the water. Therefore, the suit of Cups is receptive, peaceful, at rest rather than moving or aggressive. If a cup moves rapidly it spills the water.

In the pictures on the cards, not all the Cups have Water in them. In some no water appears at all. Blue, the color for the element, does appear somewhere in every card. In choosing his backgrounds and setting up the symbols, Hermann Haindl thought more of cups than of water. Nevertheless, as he commented when we discussed the suit, a cup not holding water is not fulfilling its purpose. If we create perfect forms and structures in our lives but these forms contain no real content of feeling, they become meaningless.

Love belongs to the entire Tarot, not just one suit. At the same time, the suit is not one-sided. It does not portray pure happiness without troubles. This is a mature Tarot. By that I mean it comes from an artist who has suffered, who has struggled to understand (and accept) pain and sorrow as well as joy. Most of these cards show some difficulty in the midst of happiness. The backgrounds are stone and water. In some of them the stone actually dominates. Some people may find this pessimistic. But joy becomes more precious when we have known suffering.

## ACE OF CUPS

The Ace is the Holy Grail itself. In the earliest Celtic legends the Grail was a stone. In some versions it appears as a disk or a tray. In most stories, however, the Grail is a cup. Christian myth describes it as the cup from which Christ drank at the Last Supper. Later, Joseph of Arimathea used this cup to collect Christ's precious blood as He bled on the cross. Joseph then took the Grail to Britain, landing at Avalon. Joseph later became wounded, and because he had come to embody the spirit of the land, the country all around him became a wasteland, a barren desert, as long as Joseph remained ill. And nothing could heal Joseph, could make him whole, until the Grail knight—Parsifal, or in some stories Galahad—achieved the quest of the Grail. For even though the land was wounded, the Grail kept it alive until that moment when the holy knight could restore the king.

**Ace of Cups in the North**

There are many interpretations of this story. Most people agree that it goes back before the Christian versions to ancient Celtic myth or ritual. Avalon—usually identified as Glastonbury—was the entrance to the Otherworld of the Fairies, the spirits. The Grail was probably the cauldron, or feeding pot, of the Great Mother. The pot was inexhaustible, always giving food to the Mother's worshippers. The image of a pot symbolizes the Goddess's womb, source of all life. The food was spiritual as well as physical, for the Mother fulfills our souls with joy as well as our bodies with nourishment. The wounded king represented the land in winter, or in times of famine. He symbolized as well the cycle of decay, death and rebirth. Rebirth came through the young knight who brings healing by giving himself to the Grail, the Mother. Remember the surrender of the Hanged Man.

In the Major Arcana we saw how kings were identified with the process of nature, especially age and decay. In some places the old king may have been ritually killed so a fresh and vital youth could replace him as the mystical lover of the Goddess. Perhaps the knight himself killed the king and took his place. Or maybe the knight was sacrificed so his vitality would heal the king. In the later Grail legends we find an element of self-sacrifice. In some stories Parsifal or Galahad leaves the world once he has achieved the Grail.

The Christian myth is more psychological than the original, partly because it comes later, and partly because Christianity is not so much a religion of the land. In recent years Neo-Pagans have pointed out that Christianity, coming from a hot desert country, is alien to the cold wet lands of Northern Europe. For a modern interpretation of the Grail story, let us say that the wounded king symbolizes our own wounded lives, our own sick souls. We struggle through our work and relationships, seeking pleasure and fulfillment, and yet something seems wrong, or empty. Life is hard and often painful. In the twentieth century the wasteland has proven a potent symbol. For many people the old values have gone, and the world seems empty, headed for destruction.

But the message of the Grail, the Ace of Cups, is precisely that the Wasteland is only half the story. The Holy Spirit has not left us but remains in hiding, still nourishing us, still keeping us alive with hope and desires for fulfillment. The old values are the wounded king. But the young knight is coming as well, for in our time we have begun to see the renewal. As we saw in the Star, Gaia is washing her hair. Not just our own individual souls, but the Earth itself, the Goddess is returning to us. It is our responsibility, as the young knight, to serve her. In Christian terms the knight who joins with the Grail is the soul who has come to Christ. In doing so, he or she restores the personal wasteland of his or her life.

Some modern writers, such as John and Caitlín Matthews, have emphasized the universal meaning of the Grail. Each of us can find our own quest, our own Grail to seek. What matters is the idea of service, giving ourselves to something greater than selfish desires. We will see this theme again, in the image of Parsifal himself, the Son of Cups.

The picture shows a simple cup formed of spiraling gold. The spiral symbolizes evolution, the spirit rising through its experiences to a higher level. This idea of experience is vital. We do not simply leave ordinary life behind in order to become holy. When Parsifal first encounters the Grail he does not respond (remember the Fool's closed mouth). This is because he has not experienced the world, especially suffering. Spiritual teachings tell us that our lives serve a purpose. They further the evolution of our individual souls, and the soul of the world. Through suffering—especially the suffering he himself causes—Parsifal discovers and accepts that he must serve the Grail.

As the Grail turns, it gives off water mixed with light. This too symbolizes the idea of development. The emotions—water—become "enlightened." A personal Grail quest shows us the truth in our lives.

A single drop falls into the Cup. In the center of the drop we see a red spot, the only red in the picture. Hermann Haindl remarks that it can be fire or blood; both symbolize life. The Christian interpretation of this drop would be the seed, or semen, of the Holy Spirit entering the material world through the womb of Mary. The Pagan version of the drop is the male principle uniting with the female. It shows the same idea, the same image, as the lance entering the Cup on the card of the Lovers.

## DIVINATORY MEANINGS

In readings the Ace of Cups symbolizes, first of all, a time of happiness. It represents the gift of love, of joy, of optimism. In questions of relationships, the Ace of Cups shows love flowing openly between the two people. As the Grail, the card is perhaps the most optimistic in the deck. For in times of suffering it tells us that happiness is possible. We may have to seek it out. We may have to make our own Grail quest. But it is there.

We can carry the idea of the quest further. The Ace may represent some important task which the person must accept and then fulfill. As with Parsifal, this may involve hardship or sacrifice. The Grail challenges us to recognize some purpose greater than our own immediate satisfaction. This meaning becomes emphasized with the Son of Cups, the Son of Stones, or the Magician.

## REVERSED

The reversed Ace of Cups means that the happiness is blocked in some way. There are painful emotions, maybe anger or jealousy. People may have trouble communicating with each other. If the card represents a quest, then reversed might indicate the person trying to deny some greater responsibility. In the most extreme situation, the reversed Ace of Cups may show somebody questioning the meaning or value of life. Remember, then, that the Grail is still there. The card still indicates the possibility of being nourished by joy.

## TWO OF CUPS—LOVE

The title of this card means love as a creative force in the world. This is why Haindl has given it the *I Ching* hexagram 1, "The Creative." Love is powerful, creative for the world as well as for individuals. Through sexuality nature renews itself, but without love renewal is meaningless. For each of us, love gives the inspiration to make something of our lives. The hexagram comes from doubling the trigram, "The Creative." That is, three unbroken lines doubled make six. The *I Ching* identifies this hexagram with Heaven (just as hexagram 2, "The Receptive," means Earth). People in love feel Heaven shining on them. But the hexagram means more than love. Like the Ace of Cups, it implies responsibility. When a person receives such "Creative Power" (Wing's title), she or he must use it for a good purpose. So love in this card becomes something more than personal happiness. We need to give the energy back to the world.

Hermann Haindl painted this peacock after his trip to India where peacocks are a powerful symbol in religion and art. As we learned in the Major Arcana, the bird symbolizes rebirth and balance. When love enters our lives we feel reborn.

The peacock here is a fantasy bird. It emphasizes the importance of fantasy in love, which is not simply a physical attraction. Eroticism involves the imagination as much as the body. The physical aspect is suggested in the graceful curve of the bird's neck, the provocative way it tilts its head and the bright colors flaring up behind it. As in the Major Arcana trump Alchemy, the left-hand-side

Love
Two of Cups

of the card is blue, the right-hand, red (or pink). They are male and female, but also active and receptive. Love requires both sides. The beak points to the left, the unconscious, while the eyes look right. Through love, unknown feelings rise to the surface.

The two cups symbolize balance. They show two people joining together in love. Each one is balanced, fulfilled, by the other. A single star pours light into the left-hand cup. Love brings light into our lives. People depressed talk of being in darkness. When love comes we feel our bodies fill with light as well as with desire. Light is a symbol of vitality and creative energy. By having all unbroken lines, the *I Ching* hexagram expresses the yang principle, that is, light.

The star is the same six-pointed star we saw in the Lovers. It represents Hagall, which reminds us of the Empress. These are two of the main trumps dealing with love. The Lovers trump indicates fulfillment in relationships, while the Empress symbolizes the power of love. But Hagall is also the Chariot, the card of will. Love is not passive. We do not just "fall" in love. Unless we choose to love, no connection between people is possible.

## DIVINATORY MEANINGS

In readings, the Two of Cups shows a relationship. Many of the same meanings apply as with the Lovers. This card is more direct, less esoteric. It shows two people joining together, helping to fulfill and balance each other. The card sometimes indicates a new relationship—one that's just beginning, or one that will start in the near future. The card can be a very exciting one to receive in a reading. If the person is involved with someone but does not know how far the relationship will go, the Two of Cups suggests that the relationship is serious, but also that the person may need to make a commitment.

## REVERSED

The Two of Cups reversed indicates trouble in a relationship. As with the Lovers card, it may show quarreling or jealousy. There may be an imbalance, with one person too dominant. In a beginning relationship, the Two of Cups reversed implies an uncertain future. The people may not be right for each other, or the relationship may not be as important as it seems. The reversed card may also indicate a lack of commitment.

# THREE OF CUPS—OVERFLOWING

If two is sufficient, three can be too much. Excessive emotion can be unstable—joyous one moment, tearful the next. The Three of Cups is still a happy one, but with suggestions of danger lurking in the waters of feeling.

The *I Ching* hexagram is 28. Wing titles this "Critical Mass," while Wilhelm calls it "Preponderance of the Great." This means a potential for greatness in a person or a situation. But this potential is confined in weak circumstances. Therefore, the situation is

Overflowing
Three of Cups

unstable and can break open. This can apply in many ways. One example, suitable for Cups, might involve a person with the capacity to love very deeply being in a relationship that lacks real feeling or commitment. Instability would come because of great emotion confined in a trivial condition.

The picture shows the three cups in an upward-pointing Fire triangle. This hints at an active force in all the emotion. As with the hexagram, we find the idea of something pushing to get out. However, the picture shows a cave. We are "inside." In other words, the card deals with a person's inner experiences, feelings rather than action. Actions may be needed to realize the potential for greatness. Action might also balance the great emotion.

The rocks at bottom are pitted, showing ancient roots in people's emotional lives. They may seem new to each person, but people have experienced the same feelings for thousands of years. At the same time, water indicates that emotions are always changing.

Stone in the suit of Cups indicates difficulties or oppositions to happiness. Here, rocks at bottom hint of danger. The large rock appears as a crocodile (in many Egyptian-influenced Tarot decks a crocodile appears on the card of the Fool). On the right we see the edge of a rock. The triangular shape resembles a shark's fin. This suggests hidden dangers.

Despite the fearful images, the card remains one of happiness. The Cups overflow with joy rather than tears. A single drop, with a hint of red, falls into the uppermost cup. It symbolizes the gift of joy. But it also can indicate that extra emotion that makes it all too much.

Two was balanced because it showed love between people. They were equal, and they helped ground each other's feelings in a physical reality. The Three is more internal, more a symbol of pure emotion.

## DIVINATORY MEANINGS

The first meaning is great feeling. The person has very intense experiences or reacts very intensely to situations. Usually, the emotions are joyous but they can also turn to tears. This is especially true in a weak or unstable situation, as implied in the hexagram. The person may need to find a way to express all that feeling in daily life.

## REVERSED

Reversed, the Three of Cups would suggest the feelings dammed up inside. A very emotional person is trying to act in a calm way. This may increase instability, especially if the card appears with such explosive images as the Tower. But if the cards show a successful development, then becoming calmer would seem the right approach. As in so many other cards, the context—the surrounding cards—tells us which way to interpret the reversal.

## FOUR OF CUPS—MIXED HAPPINESS

The background for the Four of Cups comes from a painting titled *The Dying Unicorn*. It shows an autumn scene, with falling leaves and bare branches. The image is sad, but also sweet. The *I*

**Mixed Happiness**
Four of Cups

*Ching* hexagram is 3, "Difficulties at the Beginning." It describes the possibilities of growth from a situation that appears dark and heavy. The hexagram was part of Haindl's inspiration for the card.

There is no water in the picture, though water is implied by the intense blue. Without water, the cups are useless. Plants need water to survive and so we see dead leaves. At the same time, the leaves will fertilize the ground for new life. Thus, autumn implies spring as well as winter, and the card leads us to the idea of new growth coming from a difficult or painful situation. The message is similar to the trump of Death, number 13 (1 + 3 = 4). As a Minor card, the Four of Cups is not so sweeping as the trump. It describes a more immediate situation.

Despite the sadness in the picture this is not really an unhappy card. The cups fall symmetrically, giving us a sense of peace. There is a feeling in the card of a moment in which everything is suspended and the person sees clearly what has happened and what needs to be done. The card connects to Justice as well as to Death.

## DIVINATORY MEANINGS

In discussing the Four of Cups with Hermann Haindl I asked him what he would say to someone who received it in a reading. He replied that this is a good card but you have to take the cups and do something with them. We could add that the situation may look very hard. The first thing the person would need to do is find that moment of peace and balance. Be aware of what is happening or has already happened, but step back and look calmly at everything. And then, even if the situation looks like one of loss, the card tells us we can do something with it. Action is possible and will lead to growth.

Haindl also said the card means to follow your own nature. This might be the clue to filling the cups, to using the situation in a positive way. The water is your own feelings. They need to flow openly. But four cups are not just for you alone to drink. You need to share the cups with others. Therefore, growth lies in generosity as well, and allowing others to express their feelings.

## REVERSED

Reversed, the Four of Cups suggests a loss of balance. The difficulties become emphasized, as the person finds it hard to see the possibilities. Emotions may become suppressed. If the person is negative or hopeless, the reversed card implies that this view is distorted. Remember that the card and the hexagram show positive experiences within a difficult situation.

## FIVE OF CUPS—DISAPPOINTMENT

The background of the Five of Cups shows brown rock, without water. This implies a situation where plants have not been able to grow, in other words, where hopes have not fulfilled themselves. Remember that stone in the suit of Cups symbolizes limitations. The picture says that in this situation the limitations on the person

Disappointment
Five of Cups

are powerful. We do find water in the card; it spills from four of the cups. But the water is a thin stream, a symbol of disappointment. Compare it to the flowing happiness of the Three of Cups.

The hexagram is 9, titled by Wilhelm "The Taming Power of the Small," and by Wing "Restrained." The weak line (fourth from the bottom) prevents the creative trigram (the three straight lines) from rising to the top. The hexagram suggests ultimate success, for two strong lines appear after the weak one, but not now. Now the person needs patience and a gentle rather than forceful approach.

Similar ideas are implied in the single cup at the bottom, catching the water. Things may seem lost or ruined, but something substantial remains. There is a foundation to the person's life, something solid and real that nothing can knock over or destroy. The single cup also says that experience has not been wasted. Right now, the person feels disappointed. Something she or he desired has not happened. It seems that all the effort has gone for nothing. But the water flows into the final cup. In future situations, perhaps the next time the person tries something, she will discover that the effort was not wasted after all.

We can understand this if we think of the classic Cups situation, a love affair. At the beginning it may feel like the Three of Cups, flowing with joy and hope for a new future. But now it has not worked out that way. The person feels disappointed. All that emotion, all the plans, now seem foolish. All for nothing, she thinks. The card says otherwise. She has learned from the situation. The next time there may be more honesty, or a better awareness of the other person. Remember that the hexagram indicates success in the future.

## DIVINATORY MEANINGS

In a reading we might see this emphasized if the Two of Cups appeared in some position such as Possible Outcome in the Celtic Cross. The History of such a situation could be shown clearly in three cards. The Center would be the Five of Cups, indicating current disappointment. The Basis would be the Three of Cups, while the Two would appear as Possible Outcome. The Final Outcome in such a reading might be a card emphasizing patience, or acceptance of the present situation.

Patience belongs to this card, as it does to the hexagram. This is not the best time for action. The person needs to wait for a better moment. This contrasts with the Four, which recommends direct action. At the same time, the Five calls for belief in the future. The person may find this difficult, for the card is dark at the bottom and center, while the top appears murky, like mud. This shows the person's state, in which confusion and disappointment become exaggerated. The person needs to focus on the cup at the bottom, for this is an aspect of the Ace, a cup of hope.

## REVERSED

The Five of Cups reversed shows the person paying more attention to that single cup. She or he may begin to come out of the disappointment, to look more to the future. The person gains a more realistic view of the past, seeing the good things that have come out of the situation. With various other cards it may indicate a time to consider new beginnings based on what the person has gained or learned in the past.

## SIX OF CUPS—HAPPINESS

Happiness in the Six of Cups is not pictured as overflowing emotion, as in the Three of Cups. In fact, no water appears in the Six of Cups at all. Instead, the image is one of balance and peace. The picture is asymmetrical, with four cups on one side and two on the other. They are balanced more subtly than with a rigid rule of three plus three.

The hexagram is number 58, titled "Encouragement" by Wing and "The Joyous, Lake" by Wilhelm. This is one of the eight hexagrams formed by doubling a trigram. The trigram, too, is called "Joyous." Wilhelm describes 58 as a hexagram of success and joining with friends. Friendship and family are part of the Cups suit, as important as romance and emotion.

Haindl chose the background because it seemed right to him as an expression of happiness. Once he had the picture, the arrangement of the Cups fell into place. In a sense he created the card backwards, following his reactions rather than a plan. The column on the left would seem to be natural rock. In the original painting, however, it forms part of a temple. The hole at the bottom is a window.

There is quite a bit of stone in this picture. The effect, somehow, is not grim, as in the last card. This is partly because light shines on or within the stone column, while on the right, the bubble floats gently between the cups. The bubble reminds us of similar images from the Major cards, such as the floating globe of light before the High Priestess. Similar images appear on other Minor cards. Here the bubble is delicate, clear, with a trace of red, the color of life energy to show that the situation is not static. The center is dark, or rather, reveals the darkness on the wall behind the bubble. This indicates that even in times of happiness and friendship some hidden part of ourselves remains untouched, unknown. This is the situation in the Minor Arcana, for it is only through undergoing the great challenges of the Major Arcana that we come to true self-knowledge and serenity. Still, this card represents serene moments

Happiness
Six of Cups

in ordinary life. Despite the dark center, the outer edges of the bubble glow with light.

The bubble, by its nature, is perfect yet delicate, vulnerable to being broken. Happiness can sometimes have this quality. Above the two cups shines a five-pointed star. As a symbol of the Goddess it signifies wisdom, power and protection.

As with the Major Arcana trump Alchemy, the picture is divided between a light and a dark side. And as with the trump, the left is the side of light, a reversal of the usual symbolism in which the "left-hand path" is the way of darkness. Just as light does not mean anything without darkness, so happiness needs an awareness of sadness to give it a full sense of life and understanding.

We see four cups in the left-hand column, two in the right. The number four traditionally means law, while two, as we know from the Two of Cups (and the double images on trump 6) means love.

Together, the images suggest that our lives become balanced and happy when they are filled with love, but also when they follow natural laws. When there is no excessive behavior, or exaggerated fantasies, happiness flows from a solid foundation.

## DIVINATORY MEANINGS

In readings the Six of Cups would signify a time of happiness for the person. It stresses that this happiness comes from loving others and being loved in return. It also describes the person's life as balanced and peaceful. Whether this condition remains for an indefinite time or passes, like a single perfect moment, will show in the other cards. If they indicate that happiness passes, they might give some indication why. If the person is taking happiness or other people for granted, or behaving excessively, then she or he can look for some change that will give the happiness a more solid base.

## REVERSED

The reversed Six of Cups has various possibilities. The happy moment might be passing, as if the darkness becomes stronger than the light. Or the person might not recognize the happiness that is there. Finally, reversed could suggest some unbalanced or excessive behavior that is preventing the person from finding happiness. The meanings might combine the possibilities.

## SEVEN OF CUPS—ILLUSIONS OF SUCCESS

The image on this card is very direct. The six cups pointing upward symbolize the appearance of everything going well. Neatly ordered, symmetrical, they suggest that the person's life is organized and in control. In the center, however, we see an upside-down cup. This tells us that the success and control are illusions. The center is empty.

The *I Ching* hexagram is number 4, "Youthful Folly" in Wilhelm, "Inexperience" in Wing. This carries the idea of mistakes, but not disaster. Setbacks and problems will come more from lack of experience than bad intentions. The hexagram and the picture carry

**Illusions of Success**
Seven of Cups

a quality of arrogance. The person is very proud of her or his success. She feels that everything has been done, that she has conquered the world. This is a quality of youth, but it can come at any age, when the person seems to be getting whatever she wants. The arrogance comes from an illusion, for life is not so easily conquered. There may be problems or dangers facing the person precisely at that moment of seeming victory. Remember that seven is the number of the Chariot. In that trump, the will achieves mastery over the world by confronting its deepest feelings.

None of the cups hold any water. This, too, suggests that success is an illusion. The person has achieved a great deal, only to find that these things do not bring real satisfaction. The victories are all outside, while the real core of the person remains untouched, upside down. The card appears bright, but the bottom is dark, or hidden. The background shows a desert, or perhaps a cave in a desert. The card says that the person has been chasing the wrong kind of success, that which looks good on the outside but does not satisfy the soul.

## DIVINATORY MEANINGS

In readings, the card might apply generally. That is, the Seven of Cups might say to the person, "Look deeply at what you have made of your life. It appears successful, but does it give you true joy? Do you know yourself?" The card warns against arrogance and complacency.

The card might also refer to some specific situation. Everything seems to be going well, but this may be an illusion. The person may need to look carefully at the situation, in order to avert some serious problem. On a practical level, the single overturned cup may indicate that the person has overlooked something.

Another meaning might be fantasies. The person *thinks* she or he has achieved great success, but in fact has accomplished very little. Hard work and a sense of realism may be needed to make the fantasies reality.

## REVERSED

The Seven of Cups reversed may indicate that hidden problems are emerging. The dangers come to the surface, and the person discovers that what seemed a great victory was only an illusion. However, an alternative interpretation would say that the person has become more realistic. She or he gives up illusions, or arrogance, and starts looking at what really matters. If a single cup indicates hidden problems or dangers then the person becomes aware of this and takes action. If the person has been filled with fantasies, then she or he begins to make them a reality. Notice that when we reverse the card, the outer six cups—the illusions—become overturned, while the center cup—the inner reality—becomes upright.

## EIGHT OF CUPS—FAILURE

From the great happiness of the first three cards, the Cups have been moving steadily into trouble. It is as if everything was too easy

Failure
Eight of Cups

in those early cards. Thinking life will always provide joy, a person can become arrogant, as we saw in the last card. In the Eight of Cups the process reaches its lowest point. The person experiences failure and pain. But the optimism of the suit remains. Through such setbacks we not only learn about ourselves and life, but we come to appreciate future happiness more. We do not take the gifts of joy and love for granted. The last two cards in the series, the Nine and Ten of Cups, bring us back to success, first material, then spiritual.

The *I Ching* hexagram, 41, mirrors some of these ideas. Wilhelm titles it "Decrease" and Wing "Decline." It indicates a loss. On the surface this would seem to bring pain. However, if a person accepts loss, does not try to oppose it, but simply waits peacefully for another turn of the wheel, then "supreme good fortune" will follow. The two trigrams are "Keeping Still" over "Joyous." In other words, the joy remains, but at the bottom. It needs time to rise once again to the surface.

In the picture we see lines of light, and flowing water. This carries the same idea of hidden joy that cannot be destroyed. Nevertheless, the cups are all in confusion, pointing in different directions, unbalanced with each other, as if the person's life has become chaos. What was built up, what seemed stable, has broken down. The background appears to show a rock landscape. Actually, it shows two images of barrenness and pain. Just above the middle we see a broken pipeline. Now, a pipe is used for irrigation, or to carry water to a town. Therefore, the broken pipe symbolizes desolation, the channels of life broken (see also the Ten of Swords). The water of joy is unable to flow from the source—the Ace of Cups as symbol of the Spirit—to our daily lives.

The other image is that of a wounded snake, with its head at the bottom of the picture (in between the two bottom cups). A line of blood appears just behind the head, while another trace of blood shows at the corner of the mouth. The snake, remember, symbolizes the Goddess, who gives joy and everlasting life to her children. But here the children have wounded her snake. In the Major Arcana card of the Devil, the snake came from a black hole and uncoiled to be transformed by the crystal into spiritual truth. Here the snake coils back in pain, and tries to re-enter the hole.

This should make it clear that this card does not refer only to individual situations. The barrenness symbolized by the broken pipeline has become very real, in places where people have overfertilized the land, or cut down the forests for profit and fuel and so changed farmland into desert. And the Devil's snake—in such horrors as death camps, or the bombing of Hiroshima, Nagasaki, Dresden, Cambodia, and so many other places, we have seen the snake uncoil from the dark hole without transforming into wisdom.

In the lower-right corner of the card we see words. The words come from a speech given by Chief Seattle (the Son of Stones) to declare the rights of Native Americans. In his speech Seattle told not only of injustices done to humans, but to the animals, and to the Earth Herself. To Native Americans—and in the Haindl Tarot—"human rights" forms part of the sacred life of our planet. Our *failure* to recognize this has brought about the chaos of the falling cups. Nevertheless, the water in the picture, and the "Joyous" in the hexagram, show that we have not lost everything. If we accept our mistakes and change our relation to our world, supreme good fortune may still come to us.

## DIVINATORY MEANINGS

In readings the meanings revert to a person's practical situation. The card may signify general failure in a person's life. More likely, it shows the failure of some special project or enterprise. The card indicates loss, but if this loss has not occurred there may still be time for the person to take a different approach. Failure may come from arrogance, or greed.

If the failure has happened, the card suggests that things may not be so bad as they seem. Not everything has been destroyed. The person needs to wait, to let things settle, and then see what remains. This is not a time to push. The person should not try to rebuild immediately. If the card refers to a love affair (Cups is the suit of love) the person should not look for a new relationship right away, but rather try to understand and accept what has happened.

This is a time to be open to others, to be humble and accept help, without shame or embarrassment.

## REVERSED

The Eight of Cups reversed emphasizes the hidden joy in the card. If some failure has occurred, then the person has come to understand it. New happiness begins to emerge. If the person is headed in some bad direction, then reversed shows her beginning to recognize this. The reversed card is a good indicator for positive change.

# NINE OF CUPS—FORTUNE

In the Nine of Cups we see an answer to the previous one. The chaotic eight cups have been set in order, upright and in balance. Nature has been restored and water is flowing through a hole in the brown rock. The water flows into an upright cup. Compare this to the overturned and empty cups of the Seven of Cups. Here the

Fortune
Nine of Cups

center is in balance. Furthermore, the water pouring into the cups symbolizes usefulness. People do not act excessively, they do not waste what life gives them. This is a card of good fortune, but it shows proper use and respect of nature.

The hexagram is 42, called "Increase" by Wilhelm, and "Benefit" by Wing. This comes after hexagram 41, "Decrease," emphasizing the idea that failure does not destroy but shows us how to value ultimate good fortune. The hexagram is one of wealth and happiness. In contrast to 41, which advised patience and stillness, hexagram 42 urges action. In Wilhelm's famous translation, "It furthers one to cross the great water." This matches the idea of usefulness. The hexagram advises sacrifice. Those who experience good fortune at this time should give to those who do not. Most spiritual traditions describe charity as a primary virtue. Genuine charity is seen as a way of atoning for sins. On a personal level, giving helps break down inequalities among friends, while in society the sharing of wealth increases prosperity for everyone. Hexagram 42 also describes moral increase. It tells us to imitate the good in others in order to increase it in ourselves.

The picture shows water breaking through a hole in the rock. Through the hole we also see blue sky. The image of a desert being renewed reminds us of the Star, where the fresh water flows over the rocks. Water brings life, food, joy, pleasure. The card shows us that these things, and not vast amounts of money, constitute true wealth.

The picture also depicts an emotional breakthrough. Repression and lack of feeling are often symbolized by stone. For the water to break through suggests the heart opening and long-buried feelings pouring out. The water flows into a cup. The emotions are useful, the person does something with the great surge of feeling. Reconciliation becomes possible, or a new sense of purpose. The blue sky symbolizes hope and joy.

The picture resembles a place near the Dead Sea known as Nahal David. This is a hidden waterfall where young David hid from King Saul, when the king's jealousy had driven him into a killing rage. The waterfall is invisible until you actually come upon it. To get there, you must climb over barren rock with hardly a trace of life. If, like Saul, we care only for power we will remain in the desert. But if we seek the heart of life, like David, then the water of renewal will break through the rocks.

## DIVINATORY MEANINGS

In readings the Nine of Cups signifies its title—fortune, wealth. The wealth can be emotional. The water of happiness flows in the person's life. If the person has had problems, the card signifies a breakthrough. The person's life becomes renewed. This meaning becomes emphasized with the Major Arcana card of the Star.

Whether material or emotional, the success is meant to be shared. The card advises generosity and openness.

## REVERSED

Reversed, the Nine of Cups can mean that the person tries to hoard his or her good fortune. By not sharing there is a danger of loss. Emotionally, the person has not allowed the water to break through. He or she is playing the role of Saul rather than David.

## TEN OF CUPS—SUCCESS

The Ten of Cups is more complex than the Nine of Cups. There are dark and disturbing elements in it, such as the rock rising from the water, or the stone-like clouds filling the sky.

The hexagram is 46, called by Wilhelm "Pushing Upward" and Wing "Advancement." In the card we see stone pushing up from the surging sea. The hexagram tells us that a climb in life requires an effort of will, but that this brings success. We should not confuse willpower with aggression. The hexagram advises us to seek the help of those already successful. It also advises being adaptable, like wood. The effort is to rise through virtue rather than force or cunning.

In the card stone replaces the wood of the hexagram. Since stone is more long-lasting, it symbolizes the essence of the individual personality, that which rises from the shapeless sea of life. The card recalls the Chariot riding on the wild waves. In discussing this card Hermann Haindl said that success in life is not something light and simple, but a dark and powerful force. People who find a real purpose in life find themselves carried along. And yet, they need to assert themselves as well. They need to consciously shape their own actions and events around them if they wish to fulfill that purpose. This is part of the esoteric meaning of the evolution of the individual soul. The self, but also the world, becomes transformed—evolved—through each being's effort.

The clouds hint at a situation where success brings some sadness as well as joy. Again, if people try to follow a true path in life they may find it brings them suffering. And yet, once they recognize that path, they know that happiness is not the only goal.

The rock is ancient. We see a dark hole in the center, signifying mystery. Even for those who seek to fulfill a purpose, much of the path and its meaning remains hidden. In front of the rock we see

**Success**
Ten of Cups

black dirt. This may appear grim, but in fact black dirt is best for plants. The Tarot is for nature as well as people. Success does not mean only personal satisfaction, but the restoration of life.

## DIVINATORY MEANINGS

In readings, the card indicates a successful development of the situation. This may require some effort by the person, but success is definitely indicated. There may be some clouds hovering over the situation, some unhappy consequences of success. However, other, simpler cards can balance this. The Ace of Cups, or the Six of Cups, would emphasize happiness. In its broadest sense the card indicates finding a path in life. It shows that a person is fulfilling a purpose. This may not be easy, but the person is moving in the right direction.

## REVERSED

The Ten of Cups reversed suggests something blocking the person's success. As we saw with the card of the Universe, the block may be outside—opposition from others, a difficult situation—or it may come from within—negativity, apathy and so on. The hexagram suggests that an effort by the person can break through the opposition. Reversed may also indicate that the person has difficulty discovering a purpose in life (or in an immediate situation). Again, the card indicates that such a purpose exists. The person needs to recognize it.

# THE SUIT OF SWORDS

THE SWORDS REPRESENT the element of Air, which means mind. In their most positive sense they symbolize cutting through problems, separating illusions from reality, finding the true principles that govern the shifting ground of ordinary life. But Swords are also weapons, and as such they symbolize aggression, conflict, sorrow and pain.

A number of esoteric Tarot designers have depicted the Swords as the "highest" of the Minor cards. This is because they view the mind as something separate from the "gross" physical body, and truth as apart from, or even opposed to, nature. With the Sword of intellect they seek to liberate the soul to the higher realm of abstract truth. In the Haindl Tarot, truth comes from the Earth. The Hanged Man achieves liberation by returning to nature rather than escaping it.

Something else separates the Haindl Tarot from earlier decks. The Rider deck of Waite and Smith (as the best-known example) appeared in 1910, before World War I. The Haindl Tarot comes from the last quarter of the twentieth century, after both World Wars, Korea, Vitenam, Cambodia, after the death camps and the famines, after civil wars and organized massacres. With such experience behind us we cannot look at swords without recognizing their main function. A sword is possibly the first weapon designed entirely for human combat. Bows and arrows, like spears, were used for hunting. Axes and knives serve as tools. Swords exist only for heroic noblemen to battle each other.

In the Grail stories, especially the later Christian versions, the swords symbolize the knight's courage and even his legitimacy. Arthur and Galahad both pull a sword from a stone to prove their power as redeemers. Arthur uses his sword to bring unity to Britain. Galahad uses his to achieve the Grail quest and restore the wounded king. Swords, therefore, symbolize spiritual power. But pulling a sword from a stone also suggests "freeing" spirit from Earth (and freeing male from female, a renunciation of sexuality). In the Haindl Tarot we have learned to see this view of freedom as a fundamental mistake.

We might argue that the time has come to change the Swords suit into something else, in the way Haindl has changed Pentacles to Stones. But the Tarot deals with reality, not just the world we would like to see. In order to transform the energy that produces conflict, we need to recognize and examine it. The Swords are the most difficult suit, but life often is difficult. This is true for the individual as well as society. The cards in the suit express both levels. While they develop ideas about society they also show us something about ourselves. The Swords help us to see connections between our private experiences and the general condition of the world.

This connection forms one of the fundamental principles of the *I Ching*. Because the Haindl Tarot looks at political and social situations, because it shows the fate of the Earth and not just of the individual, it comes closer to the *I Ching* than many earlier Tarot decks. The Three of Swords is an example. In the Rider deck and others it depicts sorrow, the image of a heart pierced with swords. In the Haindl Tarot we see an image of "mourning" for the world's suffering. This does not mean the card cannot represent individual pain. It simply sets that pain within a wider context.

Even more than with the other suits the *I Ching* here does not just give additional information. The hexagrams form a necessary part of the entire meaning. In general, they give a somewhat more optimistic view than the cards themselves. This balances some of the Swords' negativity. The hexagrams balance the cards in a more subtle way as well. Because a sword exists only for warfare it lacks a connection to nature (a spear hunts food, a cup holds water). The element of Air, while an essential part of life, still takes us away from the Earth. The hexagrams deal with the cycles of the seasons, with the barren land in winter, the revival in spring, with the rise and fall of light.

We should remember that the Swords are only one suit. Because we find suffering so difficult we tend to overemphasize it. This becomes apparent when we do readings for people. If one problem card appears in a very optimistic reading, many people will go away with the single image fixed in their minds. We need to look at Swords as only one aspect of life, one viewpoint of the world around us.

The swords in the pictures are the only emblem Hermann Haindl has taken from actual objects. Because of the importance of swords to the European aristocracy, many beautiful examples exist.

Haindl chose the swords of the Alamannen, a Germanic tribe who lived along the southern Rhine in the period after Christ. As objects famous for their perfection, their swords demonstrate the terrible duality of this symbol. They show people's dedication to making beautiful things, highly technical and elegant as well. This represents the achievement of intellect. And yet, they kill people. We find the same problem today. Some of the world's brightest scientists and engineers devote their time to developing more and more sophisticated devices that can serve only one purpose—the extinction of all life on Earth. The time has come to find uses for intellect that will serve the world and not destroy it.

## ACE OF SWORDS

This link to the Egyptian court cards shows the primordial creation scene of Egyptian myth. In the beginning there was only Nun, the chaotic waters. We find the same idea in the Bible, with "darkness on the face of the deep." From Nun, a single hill emerged. Some texts call this hill Atum, others describe Atum as a God who lived on the hill. Now, the water, Nun, represents the female principle, and the hard hill, Atum, the male. From this union the first Gods were born, and through them the universe.

To this powerful scene Hermann Haindl has added the blade of the sword coming down from above to touch the hill. Since Swords/Air represents intellect, the image suggests the divine mind activating nature, a scene similar to the Michelangelo painting in the Sistine Chapel, where a spark leaps from the fingertip of God to the finger of Adam. Here, too, we see a light on the tip of the sword.

In the Aleister Crowley Tarot and the Rider deck of Waite and Smith the Ace of Swords shows a sword pointing up to pierce through a crown. This symbolizes the mind piercing through nature to eternal truth. In this picture the sword points down, the descent of sacred light into nature. We see the beginnings of green plants on top of the hill. This shows us that the Spirit is not abstract intelligence but the giver of life.

The Ace of Swords is the gift of Air, the mind as intellect and creative force. Christianity calls this the Logos, the Word of God, the Word as God, creating the universe. In the picture the sword has

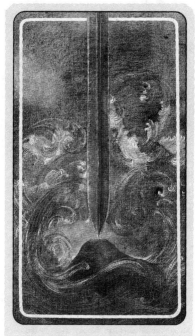

Ace of Swords in the South

stirred up the water into waves. Water is the receptive, the potential for life. It needs the active force to bring something real out of that potential.

Haindl originally painted this card before his trip to Egypt. When he and Erica were there they visited Mt. Sinai, climbing to the peak to see the dawn. They realized at that moment that the hill on this card is Sinai as well as Atum. Since we have seen that the Father of Cups is Moses as well as Odin, this makes another connection between Water and Air.

In terms of individual psychology the water symbolizes the imagination, with its great creative possibilities. Without intelligence, this possibility remains vague and formless.

Intellect, however, is equally useless, or even dangerous. Until water rises into the air as vapor, the air remains arid, empty. So if human beings act in the world from logic alone, without feeling or intuition or an awareness of sacred truths, they become destructive, the swords as weapons. The point of the sword just touches the hilltop. This represents a balance between the two forces. A little lower and it will pierce the hill, as if cutting into the breast of the Mother. Many tribal peoples have seen Western technology as exactly this, a blade cutting into the body of the Mother.

The Tarot does not reject Logos. On the contrary, with all its symbols and ideas, the Tarot shows the value of intellect. But the mind needs balance. It needs that inner base of Spirit. Human intelligence cannot act on its own but must receive the divine spark, and then act to develop the truth in human terms. As examples of this process Haindl has cited Moses receiving the Law on Mt. Sinai, Odin receiving the Runes at the base of the World Tree, and the Egyptian hieroglyphs used to create the sacred books. On an individual level art seeks a similar balance in order to convey truth. The painter or writer needs technical skill, but also genuine inspiration. The card shows us art as well as nature, for the way the waves rise up, with swirls and curlicues like ornaments, shows the deliberate creation of the intellect.

The Sword divides things. It divides Heaven and Earth, male and female, light and dark, mind and nature. Such division is necessary for creation, for if everything remains mixed together, the universe cannot exist. Without day and night and the change of seasons, life would not survive. Division also helps us understand the world. By dividing experience into the four elements of the Minor Arcana, we get a better grasp of ourselves. Yet all such divisions are artificial. They serve a purpose but we must not confuse them with reality. The final polarity is that between wholeness and separation. We need to find the balance between these two, to see the universe and life as all connected, while recognizing the various parts and the ways they function.

## DIVINATORY MEANINGS

In readings this card signifies intelligence. It can mean a time when the person is able to think clearly, to analyze the different sides of the situation. The person will tend to separate a problem into its parts, to examine them very logically. The card also may recommend doing this, especially if the person previously has responded only with emotion. This recommendation becomes emphasized with other cards of intelligence, especially Justice.

The Ace of Swords shows a powerful personality. This is a gift, for it enables people to deal with life effectively. However, it can also slide over into aggression. More than the other Aces, the Ace of Swords needs to balance itself with other qualities. Logic needs an underpinning of intuition; otherwise it may separate itself from reality. Forcefulness needs empathy with others; otherwise it becomes arrogant and destructive.

Since Swords are an emotional suit, the Ace may signify powerful emotions. The symbolism of the waves becomes important here. They show the wild feelings stirred up by the mind. The person may need to let the waters settle in order to look at the situation more clearly.

## REVERSED

Reversed, the Ace of Swords shows all these things out of balance. It can indicate anger, aggression, a mind that considers itself coldly logical but in fact distorts reality in its drive to dominate others or control a situation. The person may need to balance the Swords' energy with the other elements. Fire puts ideas into action, Water brings sensitivity, and Earth bases it all in the outer reality.

## TWO OF SWORDS—PEACE

The Two of Swords shows us an image of tranquillity. The two swords are suspended in air. This gives a sense, as in Justice, of peace as a perfect moment. We can also describe the cards as showing a balance between humanity and nature.

The hexagram is 11, also called "Peace" by Wilhelm, and "Prospering" by Wing. The hexagram is formed by the two primary trigrams, the Receptive over the Creative. In Tarot terms we can call this the High Priestess over the Magician. An underpinning of creative energy supports the surface tranquillity. We can also say that the Magician power expresses itself in a peaceful manner.

The *I Ching* pays close attention to the changing seasons, both for their reality and as metaphors for cycles in human affairs. This

Peace
Two of Swords

hexagram refers to the pre-spring period, when life begins to return to the land. The world feels itself in harmony. Since the trigrams "Creative" and "Receptive" refer to Heaven and Earth, the hexagram unites these two. Wing notes the necessity of regulating and controlling growth, rather than letting the crops grow wild. We see a similar idea in the Swords image. The two swords stand guard over the peace. Tranquillity is not taken for granted but protected.

We know the necessity of guarding both peace and prosperity. On the other hand, in politics necessity can become an excuse for militarism, while in relationships or work over-caution can lead to suspicion or aggression. This problem belongs to the duality of the card, expressed both in the number two, and in the idea of Peace as a quality of Swords.

The background for the picture comes from Haindl's *Dream of India* painting. It resembles the background for the Six of Cups, from the same painting. We see again a temple pavilion on the left side. Here we see two stone walls, the image of difficulties or threats to peace. From this we see the reason for the swords. Beyond the rocks we see peaceful trees in a wintry scene made silver by the Moon. At the bottom of the Moon we see a touch of red, a possible hint of war.

## DIVINATORY MEANINGS

In readings the Two of Swords means tranquillity. It speaks of achieving a sense of serenity, possibly in a difficult situation. For now, the conflicting forces are kept apart and all is quiet. The forces (the two walls) may refer to people quarreling, especially if the subject of the reading finds him or herself in the middle.

The time of peace may provide opportunities for prospering, or new growth. The person needs to take care that the proper steps are taken so that growth will continue.

## REVERSED

Reversed, the Two of Swords shows a disruption in the harmony. The opposing sides may be pushing together, upsetting the balance between them, or perhaps squeezing the person in the middle. The card may act as a warning. If a time of peace has come, the reversed card may suggest that the person is not taking full advantage of it.

If the person feels embattled right now, the Two of Swords reversed might imply that he or she could bring about peace but is not doing so. The need may be to seek tranquillity within in order to produce it in the world outside. The key lies in uniting the Magician below and the High Priestess above.

## THREE OF SWORDS—MOURNING

Though the title of this card might suggest some loved person dying, it refers to a wider sense of sorrow. The mourning is for the world's suffering, and especially for young people killed in war. In

**Mourning**
Three of Swords

the Swords cards we find the influence of Hermann Haindl's own time in battle and as a prisoner of war. The cards show us the need to confront such experiences and come to terms with them. Those who have not seen these things themselves still need to recognize the reality of the outside world and its suffering.

The hexagram is 33, "Retreat" in both Wing and Wilhelm. When faced with an impossible situation there is no shame in pulling back. Retreat may be a necessity. This does not mean flight; retreat is an orderly process. Wing tells us that we should persist in small matters even if big enterprises must wait.

The hexagram does not take its image from military situations so much as from the seasons. The opposite of the last hexagram, this one indicates late summer, when the light has begun to retreat and we know that autumn and winter are coming. In such a time it makes no sense to plant crops. So in situations of sorrow it makes no sense to pretend that everything is all right. And in times of weakness it makes no sense to start massive projects or mount great opposition to external problems. First we need to experience the winter. Then the natural cycle will turn again to strength and joy.

The background shows a detail from the bat we saw in the Ten of Wands. That card symbolized oppression, with the possibility of transforming the energy into liberation. The overall painting conveys the same idea. Haindl painted it to show unhappiness. At the same time, he conceived another, more subtle theme in the picture: the defeat, or end, of the patriarchal culture, which bases itself on war and subjugation. The card, therefore, shows personal pain but also a problem in the world around us. Ultimately it urges us to seek an understanding of the relationship between our own sorrows and those of the world, between personal pain and political oppression.

The detail is so close we lose a sense of the original painting. This indicates a condition of mourning. We see only the pain and lose our knowledge of the wider events of our lives. In the middle of the picture we see a wound. From it a single tear falls. The water emerges as a clear bubble, a symbol of the purification that comes through suffering.

## DIVINATORY MEANINGS

In readings the Three of Swords is clearly a difficult card. In the Haindl Tarot the Three of Swords may refer to oppressive situations around the person, even political conditions making life difficult. More commonly it will indicate some personal sorrow. The card reminds us that such experiences are part of life and we can get through them if we accept this. The mourning may be for an actual person if someone important to the person has recently died. However, the reader of Tarot cards should never look at this card (or any other) as a prediction of anybody dying. An attempt to predict death shows arrogance in a Tarot reader. Since the chances are great that the reader has misunderstood the message, he or she will likely instill terror for no reason.

The Three of Swords refers to sorrow for the loss of something. This can be a relationship, ambition, idealism or any number of things. Usually the subject of the reading will identify the specific problem. The card deals more with the emotion and how to go

THE SUIT OF SWORDS □ 75

through it. Just as light darkens, so it returns. The other cards will suggest ways of dealing with sorrow. Perhaps the person needs to balance the emotion with a wider view of the good things in life. Or else he or she can seek to understand the experience in order to transform it.

## REVERSED

Reversed, the Three of Swords shows the person having difficulty accepting the loss or sorrow. This can prolong the pain. He or she may try to keep very busy or go to parties, or else claim it doesn't matter. If so, he needs to look more honestly at feelings. In this way he can travel through the experience until the natural cycle brings renewal.

## FOUR OF SWORDS—TRUCE

As with the Two of Swords, we see a calm moment in the Four of Swords, though with more hints of difficulties. Two swords point up, two down, indicating opposing sides, or opposing energies balancing each other. Also as with the Two, the swords hang suspended in the air, creating a feeling of unreality, or of waiting for something to happen. A leaf falls to the ground, though with a feeling of moving very slowly, as if time has almost stopped. We get a sense of holding our breath. Resting on the leaf we see a pearl, or perhaps a bubble, for it appears partly transparent. This symbolizes the preciousness of a truce, or a moment of calm, in times of trouble.

The hexagram, 24, is more optimistic. Instead of a truce it shows a definite movement away from troubles. Wilhelm titles it "Return," and Wing "Repeating." Once again it refers to the cycles of nature. The particular moment is the winter solstice. The shortest day of the year, it still marks the point at which the movement changes from increasing darkness to increasing light. Wilhelm tells us that in China the winter solstice bears the title "Victory of the Light" (in a novel of mine the winter solstice is called "the Rising of the Light"). We see this idea in the hexagram, where a single yang line at the bottom shows the light making its return.

**Truce**
Four of Swords

Wing cites this hexagram as a good time for people to work together for a common goal. Wilhelm stresses that a difficult time is passing and we need to treat delicately the return of good health or the return of understanding after a quarrel. This point becomes emphasized when we remember that the card comes between "Sorrow" and "Defeat." We need to take care that the truce does not give way to another battle. Therefore, we need to nurture understanding and use the truce as a step to restoring real harmony.

In the picture we see a scene deep in the woods, presumably in winter for the trees are bare. On the right, behind the border, we see a red gash on the tree, a sign of battle. We also see a dark hole in the trunk. At the bottom of the picture a white feather appears, as if in a hole in the stone. The feather symbolizes peace. Stuck in the ground, it can symbolize peace being stifled—or peace being established, not blown away. To a large extent, the choice is ours.

The card gives a sense of silence, without animals or wind. Everything is suspended, as if waiting for that moment when the leaf touches the ground. What will happen at that moment? Will the battle start again? Or will life return to normal after the silence? A lot depends on how we make use of this time.

## DIVINATORY MEANINGS

In readings the Four of Swords indicates a moment of quiet and peace after quarrels or difficulties. If people have been battling, the card shows the quarrels dying down. The question now becomes whether real peace will come, or the people have stopped from weariness and will go back to their problems. The other cards will help indicate if steps need to be taken now for a good development, or if the situation is moving to a good result all by itself and the person only needs to allow it to unfold.

## REVERSED

Reversed, the Four of Swords shows a movement away from silence and peace. As with the card right side up, this movement can go toward new beginnings or back to troubles. If the other cards indicate the second, the reader might discuss this with the person, helping him or her to find alternatives. Sometimes it helps to ask directly what the person can do to cultivate new growth.

# FIVE OF SWORDS—DEFEAT

In most Tarot decks the Five of Swords is one of the most difficult cards. The idea of defeat can apply to many things beyond the narrow concept of a battle and a loss. It can mean the defeat of hope, of ambitions. In a wider sense the card symbolizes the defeat of nature through human destruction. In such a defeat there are no winners. Notice that the perfect swords of the Allemannen have all broken. Among other things, the swords represent modern technology. If we bring about a genuine collapse then the technology that produced it will end up falling apart as well.

Defeat
Five of Swords

The *I Ching* hexagram, number 47, provides a slightly more positive outlook. Wilhelm titles it "Oppression" and Wing "Adversity."
The commentary tells us that the negative lines hold down the positive. Despite the bad situation, however, Wilhelm says that "cheerful-
ness" and "perseverance" will bring success. If the person remains
stable in him or herself and steadfast in goals, this can "overcome
fate." Wing, too, recommends "dedication and courage." He says
as well that the individual should give in to the mood of the times.
This idea is a very important one. In several hexagrams the *I Ching*
says the opposite. We cannot oppose the general tendencies and
must retreat or wait until the moment changes to something lighter.
But here we learn that the individual can take action, can change
the situation.

The picture comes from the painting of a dying unicorn. The

unicorn is an ancient image; this particular animal looks old. It signifies an ancient part of humanity, one that goes back to a time of greater respect for the Earth and for spiritual awareness. The animal shows its teeth but there is no aggression here, for the unicorn does not eat meat and the teeth are not sharp. The unicorn symbolizes gentleness.

Symbols that represent hope or joy in other cards here become turned around. In the suit of Cups the blue sky represented peace. Here the blue sky takes on a metallic pitiless quality. In many other cards bubbles or balls symbolize new life. Here the bubble is already tainted with blood.

In the midst of such negativity we need to remember that this card represents only one vision of the world. We should remember, too, that Tarot cards, unlike *I Ching* hexagrams, do not appear alone in readings. The other cards around the Five of Swords may move the meaning in different directions.

## DIVINATORY MEANINGS

In readings the card shows a situation that can overwhelm the person. The person may feel powerless to do anything. Attempts to bring change may seem, at least at first, to go nowhere. But the hexagram tells us that we should not give in to despair. If we persist in doing what we can, if we hold to our principles and beliefs we eventually will see a change.

## REVERSED

In some Tarot decks, the reversed Five of Swords remains pessimistic, emphasizing the shame that a person feels when defeated. Because the Haindl version includes the idea of courage and persistence, reversed would suggest that the situation has begun to turn around. This meaning would become emphasized with positive cards of renewal, such as the Star, but also with cards of courage, such as the Chariot.

## SIX OF SWORDS—SCIENCE

The issue of science is a difficult one, for just as science has brought life, through medical advances and other discoveries, so it also may serve a destructive mentality that threatens our very existence. Further, the term "science" does not have to refer only to technology. The card means simply an attempt to discover objective truths about the world through observation and experiment. Yoga is often called a science, for it based its exercise and meditations on a knowledge of the body/mind built up over centuries. Occultists, too, refer to their work as a science, for they consider the Kabbalistic Tree of Life (among other things) as an objective description of the universe.

The hexagram is 61, "Inner Truth" in Wilhelm, "Insight" in Wing. Wilhelm's term makes us aware of a split betwen outer and inner perceptions of the universe. The Western scientist distrusts anything personal or subjective. If he or she cannot view it experimentally, cannot measure it, the it does not concern him. Many scientists go so far as to believe that if they cannot quantify something under laboratory conditions then it does not exist. We know of this attitude in regard to such a phenomenon as telepathy. But some scientists take the same approach to very common experiences, such as emotions; since we cannot measure them, other than as changes in blood pressure or brain wave patterns, they must not exist.

On the other side we find people who dismiss any attempt to describe the world in objective terms. Everything for them depends on intuition. Some people give up any sense of skepticism. If an idea appeals to them it must be true. And if it doesn't they simply ignore it.

Wilhelm uses the expression "visible effects of the invisible." This could describe a balanced kind of science, one that seeks to understand the workings of the universe—the invisible laws and interactions—through a study of visible effects. Pursuit of truth requires openness and freedom from prejudice. Many scientists believe themselves open while actually operating from deep prejudice, such as the dismissal of spirituality, as an illusion.

The pursuit of inner truth applies to immediate situations as well as to science. In terms of conflict, or anything to do with learning and knowledge, the Six of Swords—like Justice—tells us to find

Science
Six of Swords

the reality. We need to look at things as they are, not how we want them to be. This is more difficult than we realize.

The picture shows a hand reaching to grasp a leafless branch. The branch is part of a vineyard, one of humanity's oldest cultivations. We see traces of green around the fingers and the place where the hand touches the wood. Technology can bring new life, as in the deserts. And yet, we see a darkness beneath, as of something torn or broken. At the moment technology has damaged the world. We need to use science in a more balanced way. Hermann Haindl describes this card as an evocation of science now, and its effects on the world. But notice that more swords point up than down, a sign of optimism.

At the bottom of the picture we see lines, a link to the pattern on the Two of Stones. This strikes a positive note, for that card means "Harmony." At the top of the picture we see a face. Haindl did not plan this effect, but when he worked on the picture the canvas seemed to contain the image. This face can symbolize the ancient spirituality—the invisible—that needs to underline the scientific investigation of the visible. To me, it also resembles Hermann Haindl himself (though he probably would not agree).

## DIVINATORY MEANINGS

In readings the Six of Swords stresses the need for an objective view of the situation. This meaning becomes stronger if the card appears with Justice. The Six of Swords says that the person needs to look honestly at all aspects, including his or her own behavior. Another interpretation might stress that the person takes a narrow, supposedly objective, but actually prejudiced, view. We have all met people who insist that they only recite the "facts" in an argument. In trivial situations such people annoy us but do not bring any real harm. In more serious matters their refusal to recognize their own bias can cause serious damage.

## REVERSED

We are looking at two contradictory meanings. What unites them is the ideal of objectivity. In the first meaning the person follows this ideal. In the second he thinks he does but only uses it to dominate others. Perhaps we could describe the ideal as the card right side up, and the distortion as the card reversed. The reader's intuition can help discover the best interpretation.

## SEVEN OF SWORDS—USELESSNESS

The image of faces melted together yet fixed into stone in the Seven of Swords comes from the same painting as in the Five of Swords. This aspect of the work emphasizes the idea of defeating the patriarchal power, the "useless old men," as we might call them, who arrange the world for their own benefit. While the faces signify such a system, they also represent the individual in that system. In a world empty of spiritual and human values, people feel themselves

Uselessness
Seven of Swords

useless. They know something is missing. They know they have betrayed themselves in some way. But they do not know why, or even how to find out why. And so they become depressed, angry, tired—useless.

The hexagram is 36, which Wilhelm calls "The Darkening of the Light." Once again we see the idea of a bad situation linked to natural cycles of light and darkness. Wilhelm tells us that the Chinese words literally mean "Wounding of the Bright," bringing in the idea of pain and aggression. The hexagram describes the world around us rather than our own condition. It shows a time when conditions have turned corrupt and negative. As with the Five of Swords, the individual must not succumb to the general weakness but must hold to his or her own principles.

Wing titles the hexagram "Censorship," a practice he identifies with power in the hands of the corrupt. In such a situation, he warns, the spiritual person cannot influence the outside society and must submit, at least on the surface. It becomes important not to lose one's inner values. This allows the person to wait out the situation until action becomes possible. While this clearly describes political conditions, it can also refer to more immediate problems, such as family difficulties or problems at work.

In the Tarot card we see the swords all scattered. When a society moves in the wrong direction, individual energy becomes more and more difficult. The building of weapons takes up vast amounts of resources. The faces in the stone somewhat resemble Leonardo da Vinci, who designed various useless weapons along with his more valuable achievements.

The faces are toothless. Teeth signify vitality and strength. For many people, either consciously or subconsciously, teeth symbolize sexuality. The picture shows the idea of "toothless old men" controlling the world. Taken another way, it presents an image of personal feelings of uselessness.

## Divinatory Meanings

Like various other Swords cards, the Seven is difficult, especially in readings. When such cards come up we may tend to react in horror, exaggerating their importance. With the Seven of Swords, we need to determine first of all whether the card signifies some objective situation, or the person's own perceptions. In other words, does the person face a situation where he or she lacks the power and influence to bring change? If so, he must make sure to keep his own integrity and knowledge of the truth so that he does not despair. However, the card might refer to a person's own feelings of uselessness, that "I'm no good" sense of depression that may overcome people at different times. Such a belief is often exaggerated.

The two conditions—the outer and the personal—can join together. We mentioned above how a society without values leads to individual feelings of worthlessness. In some situations, if a person is powerless, say at work or in the family, he or she can lose all sense of value. Long illness, in oneself or a loved one, can make a person feel useless. Despite rational knowledge of the disease, he or she may feel inside, "I should get rid of this. I should make it better." Tarot readings can help the person sort all this out. Where do the feelings of uselessness come from? Can the person take action? Or does the situation demand patience and a sense of integrity? Perhaps the person needs to leave in order to create a new situation with new possibilities. Leaving a useless situation is not shameful.

## REVERSED

Reversed, the Seven of Swords shows the person attempting to deal with the feelings of uselessness. Such attempts may include trying to change the situation, trying to withdraw, or trying to develop a better sense of self. Other cards can tell us if the person approaches the problem in the best way.

# EIGHT OF SWORDS—INTERFERENCE

Interference can work for good or ill, depending on the motives and the effect. When people interfere with natural processes, disaster can result. Sometimes this interference comes from selfishness, such as cutting down forests for quick profits, as Japanese lumber companies have done in the Philippines. But it also can happen when people attempt to help. The use of chemical fertilizers and "modern" farming techniques has exhausted the land in some places where people farmed successfully for hundreds of years.

The same kind of problem can happen in human relationships. People sometimes try to help when they see friends having difficulties. Sometimes this results in more trouble. But can we really do nothing when we see people in trouble?

The positive side of interference includes political action to reform dangerous or evil policies. If we see something very wrong in the world around us, we bear a moral responsibility to do whatever we can. Movements for peace and human rights give us examples of beneficial interference.

The hexagram, 21, endorses the positive view of interference. Wing titles it "Reform" and stresses that we need to let justice be administered in order to restore a proper balance to society. In our time we have seen practical applications of this principle in the demands that war criminals and human rights offenders be brought to trial.

Interference
Eight of Swords

Wilhelm calls this hexagram "Biting Through," referring to the vivid image of the lines as an open mouth with an obstruction (the yang line in the middle). "To bite through" implies vigorous action against obstacles to justice or harmony.

The picture on the Eight of Swords at first appears aggressive. However, when we look again we see that the swords do not actually cut the trees but go in front and back. The trees do appear ill. They symbolize nature in trouble, but also a sick spirituality, for as we have seen, a genuine spirituality must base itself on the reality of nature. The swords, however, do not necessarily destroy. It all depends on how we use them.

Without the trees the swords will form a chessboard, emblem of intellect. This is indeed one of the more mental cards. Just below the eight we see a triangle with a circle inside it. As in the card of the Empress, or the Hermit, this figure represents the eye of God, that is, spiritual reality concealed within the physical world and daily life. When the intellect bases its analysis and its actions on outer realities then it begins to find the way to correct behavior. Part of the purpose of the Tarot and of the *I Ching* is to help people discover these realities for themselves.

The middle of the picture appears dark and wounded, but in fact the red on the right comes from a bush. On the other side we see gold, while above and below a bright light shines on the trees and plants.

## DIVINATORY MEANINGS

In readings the Eight of Swords indicates an interfering action of some kind. By itself, the card does not say just what the person is doing or whether it will serve a worthwhile purpose. Other cards can help determine first of all the motives for action, and then whether the action will help.

The card also might signify interference from outside. This may help or damage the person. Interference can mean gossip (Wilhelm cites "tale-bearers" as the obstruction), but it also can mean help or advice when the person needs it.

## REVERSED

The Eight of Swords reversed has two possibilities. On the one hand it might show no interference. Sometimes this becomes a recommendation, the Tarot telling the person that stepping in will only make things worse. At other times, however, not interfering might be an avoidance of responsibility. The card also can indicate that the person does interfere, but with bad results.

# NINE OF SWORDS—CRUELTY

In the fearful image of the Nine of Swords we see a bird much like the fantasy peacock of the Two of Cups. Where that bird showed the grace and charm of love, this one becomes a victim to the Swords. Not only do they pierce the bird, they even cut into the

**Cruelty**
Nine of Swords

background, slashing the very picture. The bird is a fantasy, a bird of paradise. Fantasy images in the Haindl Tarot signify human culture. The picture, therefore, shows human cruelty, not the harshness of fate or the destructive power of nature. Human beings seem to act both consciously and compulsively. We know what we do, and yet at some level we act from hidden drives that push us to do terrible things. One of the swords pierces a darkness at the bottom center of the picture. All cruelty carries a quality of self-destruction. We betray ourselves and our own hopes when we follow such a path. The human mind and spirit can create a paradise, as symbolized by the bird. At bottom left, we see beads and pearls on the bird's body. In every culture we find visions of love and harmony. Our own violence constantly pulls these visions apart.

The hexagram is 6, "Conflict." It tells us how people have conflict first of all within themselves. This makes them vulnerable to danger from without. On a societal level, the hexagram describes a situation where power serves the corrupt rather than those who work for the good of the people. This distortion produces cruelty throughout society. When a society wages an unjust war, or when the economic conditions favor greed over public benefit, then crime, and violence in the home, increase. In contrast to hexagram 36 (Seven of Swords) this hexagram tells us that the good person facing such a situation should not attempt great projects or direct opposition. He or she lacks power and must wait for a change in conditions. In the classic phrase, "It does not further one to cross the great water."

In the midst of such pessimism we find a subtle indication of hope. On the lower right we see part of an arm. This image comes from a different picture, one titled "The Three Graces." Its presence here shows that love and the hope of paradise never vanish.

## DIVINATORY MEANINGS

The use of such a card in readings is difficult. To a large extent the Nine of Swords describes conditions in the greater world. When translated into someone's immediate situation it can become too extreme. At the same time cruelty does come from individual acts, and these will show in readings if they exist in reality. We should remember that this card can indicate a cruel person as much as a victim. The position will sometimes help us see whether cruelty is given or received.

Remember as well that the card may show a person's perceptions rather than reality. The person may feel like a helpless victim, while the other cards indicate the power to make changes. The reader can help the person see alternatives.

## REVERSED

Reversed, the Nine of Swords has two immediate possibilities. One is a relief from the cruel conditions. We need to look at the other cards to see if this shows a genuine change or simply a pause. If the latter, the person needs to use this time for decisions and action. The other possibility is confusion. The cruel person masks his or her behavior with seeming kindness. Manipulation produces weakness and guilt in the victim. The reading can help the person recognize the true situation.

## TEN OF SWORDS—RUIN

Despite the grimness of many Swords cards the Tarot is essentially optimistic, believing in renewal. We need to look at "Ruin" in this context. Part of the problem of Swords lies in their distortion of the greater reality. Hermann Haindl first painted this card without the blue sky above the rock. When we discussed it, we decided that such despair went against the basic message of the deck. The blueness, therefore, symbolizes the hope of renewal. We find here a connection to Aeon, card 20 of the Major Arcana. There, too, we saw the ruin of a destructive world. But in the middle of disaster, the situation already begins to turn.

Here we see a destroyed city, symbol of the modern world bringing its own ruin. But the sky is clear. In the midst of all our dangers we have begun to return to spiritual truths. The swords in the picture appear all-powerful, but when we look closely we see that the tips have broken off. Violent behavior destroys itself. We must hope that the energy will run itself out, allowing a healthier world to reemerge.

The hexagram is 29. Wing titles it "Danger," Wilhelm "The Abysmal." As one of the eight hexagrams formed by doubling a trigram, it emphasizes the trigram image of a single yang line swallowed by two yin lines. This gives the idea of negativity and weakness, since in the *I Ching* cosmology, yang should dominate. Wilhelm says that the hexagram shows a situation that is objectively dangerous—not an imagined problem—but that the person can come through safely if he or she moves cautiously. Wing describes the danger as coming from people and the immediate situation (like the Cruelty of the last card), rather than the cosmos. He adds that if the person does not compromise he can survive the situation and will even become more confident through having coped with danger.

The picture shows a broken city, leaving only catacombs below and a desert above. Traces of green, however, appear on the barren land, the hint of new life to go with the sky. We see blood, but only a few dried lines. This gives a sense of ancient troubles, a history of

Ruin
Ten of Swords

destruction. This card gives us a vision of civilization coming to an end. It reminds us of some science fiction stories of a future centuries after a nuclear war, when deserts have replaced the cities and only the ruins remain of an arrogant and reckless culture. Like Aeon, the Ten of Swords draws on prophecies and apocalyptic visions. But these visions also lead to a restoration of ancient values.

## DIVINATORY MEANINGS

The lines of rock in the Ten of Swords resembles photographs of neurons in the brain. The swords, then, symbolize pain or confusion disrupting the pathways of thought and energy. This makes the card an image of personal difficulties.

In readings we tend to deal more with this personal level of the card. It shows the person facing great troubles. Sometimes it can indicate some specific plan or hope or relationship that now seems in ruins. However, the image of ten swords suggests a whole group of problems striking all at the same time. The quality of ancientness in the card hints that the problems may have been building for some time.

As with some other cards, the reader should look to see if the Ten of Swords represents an exaggerated perception by the person. Some cards, such as more Swords, or the Tower, would represent the Ten of Swords as an objective description. However, other cards, some of the Cups or Stones, or the Magician, or the Lovers, would indicate that panic distorts the situation. Some cards would give a suggestion of what to do. The Chariot would indicate a strong stand against the problem. The Hermit, on the other hand, would suggest withdrawing to find one's own sense of self. The Hanged Man would tell us to look to a power greater than ourselves, while the Star would allow us to trust in the process of renewal.

## REVERSED

The reversed Ten of Swords indicates the troubles beginning to pass. The sense of relief from the blue sky begins to spread. The person may be exhausted and need to rest. Think of the swords as symbolizing a headache and you will get a vivid picture of the effects of the card. As with the Nine of Swords, the relief may be temporary if the person does not make some changes in the condition which originally brought the trouble. If the conditions have existed a long time, change may require a strong and very conscious effort.

# THE SUIT OF STONES

O F THE FOUR suits the Stones are the only symbols that come
from nature. The Spear, the Cup and the Sword are all human creations. This indicates the importance of the physical world
to this last suit. It also reverses the earlier tradition, where, as Coins,
the suit represented the most specifically human of the Minor cards.
Cups and Wands deal with food, Swords with life and death. But
Coins refer to commerce, which has no counterpart in nature. Hermann Haindl has changed this to Stones to focus more on the Earth
itself.

The fourth suit has gone through a number of changes in its history. Some earlier decks changed the coins to disks, a rather abstract
symbol, as if the designers wanted to disguise the fact that these cards
symbolized something so distasteful as business. In the twentieth century, many esoteric decks followed the Golden Dawn and changed
the symbol to Pentacles. This gives them a function in ritual magic.
At the same time we can wonder if these designers also found
money too lowly a subject for the noble figure of the magician. The
best esoteric decks, such as the Rider deck, have used the Pentacle
symbol while expressing questions of work, money and nature in the
specific cards. The Haindl Tarot, too, does not abandon these important issues but puts them in a wider context.

The suit of Stones represents the gift of Earth: the realities of
daily life, of work and money, of the living world and the changing
seasons, everything that is real and solid. We saw in the introduction to the Minor Arcana how the four-letter name of God sets out
the process of creation. The final letter, the element of Earth, is the
thing created. We call this manifestation, where the potential and
the thought become manifest in physical form. The model for all
such creation is the Earth itself, the source of life and truth, the fundamental reality.

The suit of Stones takes us outside our own emotions and
thoughts to act in the world. Money, work and nature are all physical facts. They also involve more than individual destiny. Like
Swords, the suit is communal, that is, the fate of the individual is
bound up with that of the community.

There is also a particular movement in this suit that teaches us a lesson in how to make progress in our lives. The middle cards tend to extremes, going from great success to failure. With the Eight of Stones, "Knowledge," a change comes. We learn the practice of moderation, of creating a solid base and then building upon it with care and wisdom. This, too, is a lesson that applies beyond the individual. It says something about economic and political progress, which often founder because they go too fast or do not base themselves upon the will of the people (a major concern of the I Ching). And it addresses our approach to nature and progress. As mentioned before, the Haindl Tarot is not nostalgic. It does not seek to turn back the clock to ancient customs. Instead, it urges us to create a new foundation for genuine progress—spiritual as well as physical—by recognizing and respecting the Earth as our Mother. To do this we seek an awareness of natural processes, but also of history, especially the history of our mistakes—our destruction of nature—compared to the history of spiritual traditions around the world. Through this base of knowledge we learn how to work (a theme of Stones) for the restoration of the world. At the end of the suit, and therefore the end of the Minor Arcana numbered cards, the Ten of Stones gives us a vision of the Earth restored and bursting with life. Even in the Major cards we do not encounter such a vision, but only the promise of it, as in the Star or the Universe.

It may seem odd to find such an image in the "lesser" cards and particularly in the most mundane suit. The Stones, in fact, are the most spiritual as well as the most ordinary of Minor cards. We have learned in the Tarot that the sacred does not exist in some separate universe but permeates our world. The refusal to recognize this fact not only causes so many of our difficulties—psychological and political as well as environmental—but also has made so much of established religion irrelevant, or even damaging, to people's lives.

Besides the Ten, two other Stones cards in particular connect us to the sacred. The Four and the Six of Stones act as gateways to a deeper reality, reminding us that the world around us belongs as well to the Great Above and the Great Below. The power in these two cards comes partly from the background, an image of the World Tree with its roots in the dark waters, but also from the Stones themselves—the patterns they form on the cards and in our minds.

# ACE OF STONES

The eagle lands on the rock. This image is as powerful as any in the Haindl Tarot. Part of the same truth as the Hanged Man and the Star, it shows us the fundamental realms joined together: the Earth and the Sky, the "ordinary" reality and Spirit, feminine and masculine, the Receptive and the Creative, dark and light, wisdom and daily life. We could almost expect the image to come out of an ancient ritual performance, with a dancer dressed as an eagle.

The eagle, the Spirit, comes *down* to the rock. We have seen how the Haindl Tarot reverses the concept of leaving the Earth behind through ascending to the sky. Among many Native Americans, particularly Plains people, such as the Lakota, the vision quest includes the idea of ascent. According to Black Elk, men go up to a mountain, women to a hilltop. The eagle represents God because it dwells in the air, and light because it flies up into the Sun. But the person who receives the vision does not use this as a vehicle to leave the world. Instead, he or she returns to the daily life of the tribe. The purpose of a vision is to make the man or woman a whole person, able to experience the world more completely. The vision therefore descends to the person.

The Ace of Stones is the gift of the Earth, but it is also the gift of vision. This is the clue to the Haindl Tarot, this joining of realities. Traditionally this suit, as Coins, or Pentacles, has meant wealth and prosperity as well as nature. But wealth is more than money. It means a good life. The rock here is bare, like that of the Star. The Earth is soft and green, but without flowers or trees. The image is one of simplicity, showing what really matters, the Sky, the Earth, the rainbow as the universal symbol of beauty and gifts—and the Spirit beings who fill the world but remain invisible to those of us who refuse to recognize them. We can see these beings as colored lights flickering over the card. The same lights will appear in the sweat lodge "when the medicine man is strong," as Erica Haindl says. The medicine man manifests the power in the visible world. Manifestation is the gift of this Ace.

Today most Native Americans live in poverty, not by choice but from four hundred years of colonial oppression. Yet their traditional cultures did not seek out vast wealth, especially in North America. The highest value went to a spiritual relationship with the Earth.

Ace of Stones in the West

This value has not disappeared. Recently in the United States a high court ruled that the U.S. government illegally drove a tribe of Native Americans from their land in the nineteenth century. As compensation the courts awarded the tribe a vast amount of money, enough to make every one of them rich. The Native Americans refused. They want their land and will continue to fight for its restoration, despite the seeming hopelessness of victory (the land includes major cities which would come under tribal law if the land belonged officially to the Native Americans).

The eagle is an aspect of Wakan-Tanka, usually translated as "Great Spirit." We see in the eagle the same colors as in the Spirit beings: white on the top and the tail features, gold on the beak and claws, red on the wings. A line in the Ghost Dance (the central ritual of Native American revival in the late nineteenth century) says,

"Wambli galeshka wanna ni he o whoe." In English this reads, "The Spotted Eagle is coming to carry me away."

The rock is like the cosmic bubbles on so many of the other cards. It fills the same place in this card as the ball of light in the High Priestess. Erica Haindl has pointed out that if you look at it long enough, the rock begins to turn, just like the ball of light. But a rock is a natural object, something hard and real. The symbol of potentiality, of new life in so much of Hermann Haindl's work manifests here as the rock of reality. The Ace of Stones signifies the way Haindl has manifested his own vision in his Tarot.

## DIVINATORY MEANINGS

In readings this powerful card represents the good things in life—health, prosperity, beauty, even good weather if the reading should concern something where weather is an issue. It shows that these things come to the person at this time in her or his life as a gift. The person needs to recognize this and to use the gift in a positive way so as not to waste it. The card implies finding a greater truth, even visions, in daily life.

## REVERSED

Reversed, the Ace of Stones does not indicate sickness, poverty or bad weather. The gift remains but the person tends not to appreciate it. The person becomes materialist in the narrow sense, valuing the objects rather than their meaning. The reversed Ace of Stones can show conflicts over money or prosperity.

## TWO OF STONES—HARMONY

This picture comes from Hermann Haindl's painting of Dionysus. Specifically the detail derives from a section of the painting meant to indicate harmony. Harmony does not come from some static state or perfect symmetry, for such a condition never exists in the real world. Instead, it follows from an exchange of energy.

**Harmony**
Two of Stones

Harmony is constantly shifting and re-forming. We see black and gold lines flowing together. The lines actually are woven into a cloth, the "tallis," or prayer shawl, of Jewish men.

The hexagram is 16, which Wing calls "Harmony" and Wilhelm "Enthusiasm." The two titles go together nicely, showing how people can become enthusiastic without separating themselves from others or trying to control them. Enthusiasm harmonizes when it inspires rather than commands. The upper trigram signifies movement, while the lower signifies divinity. Therefore, Wilhelm says, the strong line receives enthusiasm from the five weak ones. To do this a leader must act both in sympathy with the spirit of the people and in harmony with natural law. Wing describes this hexagram as showing a time of personal charisma.

The hexagram belongs to the beginning of summer, a time when we most enjoy the gifts of the Earth. At this time thunderstorms—which the ancient Chinese saw as a manifestation of the Earth's power—bring a sense of relief and joy. People make spontaneous music in harmony with nature.

Just as the tallis fabric shows dark and light lines moving together, so we see darkness and light in the picture. On the right, the fabric forms a hole. This signifies mystery, the unknown source of life. It represents the uterus and the grave, the two gates to the other world. Haindl compares it to the hole shown on the Devil card. Opposite the hole, on the upper left, we see bright light. There is also light below and on the sides. Of the two stones, the upper is darker than the lower. This recalls hexagram 11 from the Two of Swords, where the Receptive over the Creative signified harmony because the natural movement of each blends them together.

## DIVINATORY MEANINGS

In readings the Two of Stones signifies its title—harmonic situations, good relations between people. The card is a good indicator for business or other activities that involve people working together. It recommends a harmonizing approach; it tells us to work with others rather than alone, to inspire rather than command. This is an exchange of energy going on between people, and the person has the power at this time to ensure that the exchange goes smoothly.

## REVERSED

The reversed Two of Stones shows disharmony beginning to develop. Unless the card becomes reinforced by other, more difficult cards, such as some of the Swords, it should not mean that the disharmony has reached a point of collapse. Nevertheless, something is beginning to separate. The person needs to make a special effort to restore harmonious action, whether between people or between aspects of a situation. In some situations, the other cards, or the reader's intuition, may suggest that restoration cannot be achieved. Loss of harmony does not necessarily mean disaster. The time for people to move together may have passed. It may be time now for the person to be or to act alone.

## THREE OF STONES—WORK

Just as the Ace showed the visionary aspect of the material world, so the Three of Stones takes a special approach to work. At the same time we see some difficult images in the cards, for work is a difficult subject. Without it people feel useless, even if they are financially supported. Yet work for many people is empty, even degrading. The balance in the picture indicates the need to balance work with spiritual seeking.

This seeking also forms a kind of "work." Alchemists refer to transformation as "the great work." According to Idries Shah, the Sufis describe spiritual activity as work. And the example of the shamans shows us that such seeking can be harder work than any job. The background for this picture comes from a painting of Odin on his tree. The painful sacrifice to achieve the Runes formed Odin's own great work.

The hexagram is 13, which Wing calls "Community" and Wilhelm "Fellowship with Men." Hermann Haindl chose this hexagram to indicate that the card deals with a communal issue as well as private concerns. In a society where many people face a choice of unemployment or meaningless jobs, work becomes a central issue. Wing tells us this hexagram advises recognizing other people's importance in the general community. Like the last card it does not advise individual action, or separation from society.

Wilhelm describes the hexagram as a complement to 7, "The Army." There, the one firm line among the yielding lines showed a leader. Here the many are strong, and the individual needs to give way. This does not mean surrender of principles.

The background depicts a cross. The vertical line of Spirit is strong, but the horizontal line of daily life has become overgrown with fungus. This indicates chaos in society. The painting is the same as that on the Eight of Cups, where we saw the words of Chief Seattle (Son of Stones). Chaos and destruction come when we separate human needs and economic goals from the needs of the Earth. At the same time, the cosmic balls (one on the left in front of the tree, and part of a large one behind the tree on the right) show the possibility of great change.

We saw in the Major Arcana the many significances of the number three. Linked to a cross, it reminds us as well of Christ and the three nails through his hands and feet, as well as the three days he

Work
Three of Stones

lay in the tomb. Therefore, three can mean suffering. But it also means the trinity, and the Empress, and therefore creativity. Three is the principle of manifestation, for it combines the great poles of one and two. Creativity manifests itself through work. This does not refer only to artists but to all those, such as farmers or builders or weavers, who create something real in the world through their own efforts.

## DIVINATORY MEANINGS

In a reading the card deals with work. Usually, when it appears right side up it indicates that work goes well and brings satisfaction. The spiritual aspects indicate that the work leads to the person's development. Sometimes the card may focus on the person working on her or himself. Since the card carries indicators of trouble as well as achievement its character in a reading depends somewhat on the other cards.

### REVERSED

Reversed, the Three of Stones would indicate that the work does not go well. It could signify unemployment, or work that brings no satisfaction. It could also show mediocrity in work, or in other aspects of life. This may come from laziness, or from a person not wanting to make a serious effort. It may represent a person hesitant about taking on a major project.

## FOUR OF STONES—THE POWER OF THE EARTH

The title of this card takes us back to the archaic idea of nature as a mystical force. We see in the Four of Stones the base of an ancient tree, with roots sinking into darkness. It could be Yggdrasil, the World Tree, with its roots in the hidden underworld and its branches in heaven.

The hexagram is 51, which Wilhelm calls "The Arousing" and Wing "Shocking." A double hexagram, it repeats the trigram "Arousing, Thunder." Like hexagram 16 on the Two of Stones, it describes thunder as a great shock coming from the Earth, like the voice of God. So powerfully does the Earth boom that people become terrified. Yet in summer a thunderstorm can also bring joy. The hexagram tells us that if we understand our fears we can overcome them. In a more modern society, with most people living in cities, the Earth seems less fearsome. We have our electric lights and our cars and our concrete to separate us from nature—which we experience only in parks or on holiday. But the Earth is mighty and still untamed, as we know from the great storms that occasionally strike our cities. Fear for the Earth can lead to respect and honor.

The background for the Four of Stones comes from the same painting as the Seven of Wands, and the Ten of Cups, where we saw rocks in water. The roots of the tree are red, white, yellow and blue. They represent the four directions, which in turn signify the Earth's

The Power of the Earth
Four of Stones

power, physical and spiritual (see also the introductions to the numbered Minor Arcana cards and the Court cards). For the Native
Americans each direction of the compass carried different qualities,
such as light, darkness, healing, warmth or cold, the seasons, and so
on. The people experienced these things and understood their own
place in the world. The tree represents the vertical axis joined to the
horizontal level of the directions. Also called the "center," it links
Above and Below with before, behind, right and left. The top of the
tree and the end of the roots are both not visible.

The name of this card in German, *Irdische Macht,* links it to the
Ir (Yr) Rune from the Tower. Szabo, following Spiesberger, calls this
Rune a "Rune of the Earth." But as we have seen with that card,
the Rune can also mean "to err," a symbol of the Rune's link to
atomic energy.

The strips across the tree are mists rising from the water. They signify creative ideas, which often seem foggy or confused until we examine them in the light.

## DIVINATORY MEANINGS

Signifying the Earth, the Four of Stones is one of the least personal in the deck. When we consider it for readings we have to do some translating. The card calls us to respect the sources of power in our lives. It is a card of creativity and new ideas. The person may feel overwhelmed by the energy of a situation. If she feels afraid she needs to respect that feeling. The four directions tell us to orient ourselves in the situation, to see how the different parts contribute to the whole, and to find our own place. This is a very powerful card, with the ability to take us beyond the usual experience of the Minor cards. In meditation, and with such cards as the Hanged Man, the Universe and the Ace of Stones, it can give us a glimpse of the true shamanic vision.

## REVERSED

Reversed, the Four of Stones indicates losing a sense of place, feeling confused and frightened. The person senses the powerful forces at work at the moment, but does not know where she or he fits in the situation. Action becomes difficult and the choices fearful. Many tribal peoples have based their understanding of the world on the shape of the land. A mountain or some other important feature became the physical center around which they organized their survival as well as their spiritual knowledge. When some conqueror, such as the United States or Australian governments, forced them to relocate, they became lost. The reversed Four of Stones shows something of this problem in an immediate situation.

## FIVE OF STONES—MATERIAL DIFFICULTY

The Five of Coins, or Pentacles, is often one of the more difficult cards in the suit, signifying troubles or illness. The Haindl Tarot gives this card a more fundamental meaning. In the Five of

**Material Difficulty**
Five of Stones

Stones we see a winter scene, with dead or dying trees. Winter, too, is a part of the cycle of our lives, while death is something we need to accept. The background comes from a painting Hermann Haindl painted at a time when some people refused to talk of death, even to see it. We still, in many places, follow the practice of putting makeup on corpses to make them look as they did when alive. However, in the past years a movement has begun that seeks to look at death in a more honest, spiritual way, drawing on mythology and ancient teachings as well as modern psychology. It is important to remember that the card does *not* mean only death, just as it will not appear in readings only in winter. It means life's hardships and how we deal with them.

The hexagram is 23, "Deterioration" according to Wing, "Splitting Apart" according to Wilhelm. The hexagram shows the dark lines rising to overcome the final light line. In such a situation one should avoid major initiatives or an attempt to influence the outside world. If relationships have suffered from misunderstandings or bad feelings, one should not try to repair them at this time. Instead, one should wait for a moment when the forces (patterns) in the world favor growth and harmony.

Such recommendations appear to be deeply pessimistic, but this is only if we expect that the world will always favor us. The hexagram —and the card—do not describe these conditions as permanent. If we understand and accept the Oracle's fundamental message of change, then we remember that spring does come after winter, and that winter, too, fulfills its place in the movement of the year.

We see in the Five of Stones dead or dying trees before a pool of stagnant water. The stones have no apparent pattern. They float in the air without purpose or direction. The center tree shows a red spot, or perhaps a red ball. We can see this as a wound, or even the marks made by humans as they try to save the tree. More symbolically, we can think of it as life energy at the center of the dark time. On the right a fire glows, bringing warmth and lighting up the bottom of the stones. The trees are in darkness but the sky and ground are light.

At the top of the picture, pointing down to the center, we see a feather from a white bird. In the original painting the bird's head appears diseased, like the trees. Here we see only the pure feather, like the beauty of winter.

## DIVINATORY MEANINGS

In readings the Five of Stones signifies a wintry time, when things do not go well for the person. There may be money troubles, a possibility of ill health, feelings of isolation. These things may become modifed by other cards, or by the position. If the Five of Stones appears in a place such as Hopes and Fears, it indicates the person's anxieties about such troubles, rather than actual troubles. In connection with the Hermit, the High Priestess or other such cards, the Five of Stones says that the patterns do not favor action. Looking into the self can awaken wisdom. In connection with cards like the Sun or cards indicating success or gain (such as the following card) the Five of Stones would indicate only a temporary setback.

### Reversed

Reversed, the Five of Stones indicates beginnings of movement for the better, as if in the middle of winter we see the first signs of spring. The person still may need to wait, or to act very cautiously, for the basic situation has not yet changed, and pushing can bring another setback.

## SIX OF STONES—SUCCESS

In the Six of Stones we see the opposite of the previous card, from the low to the high. The card indicates joy, wealth, great achievements. We also see the pattern for Hagall, with the hole in the middle providing the center point for the axes. When we remember that Hagall means a snowflake (as well as a hailstone) we see that the great development of this card comes out of the low point of the previous one.

The hexagram is 55, "Abundance" for Wilhelm, "Zenith" for Wing. Wing compares it to the full Moon, or the longest day of the year, while Wilhelm links it to a glorious civilization. There is a sense of sadness about all these things, for we know they cannot last. After that long day, the light begins to lessen as the world moves towards winter. But the *I Ching* tells us to rejoice in the moment. The sage, Wilhelm says, should shine like the sun at midday.

The picture comes from the same painting as the Four of Stones. It carries some of that same ability to lead us to a deeper awareness of the patterns behind daily life. The simplicity of the setting recalls the Star. Again we see primarily rock and water, the two feminine elements. However, we can also see signs of metamorphosis. If we look at the lower-right corner, we see that the rock changes to the roots of a tree, so that the wall on the right hand side can also be a trunk.

The stones form two triangles, an upper and a lower. These form the top two triangles of the Kabbalistic Tree of Life (see the commentary for the Lovers*). The center of the figure, however, is not a stone but the hole in the cave. A golden light shines through the hole (compare this to the Hermit, or the Moon). This does not

---

*See Volume I.

**Success**
Six of Stones

signify emptiness at the core, or the idea that our joys and successes are meaningless. On the contrary, the light tells us that we can find the true source of meaning, the glorious nothing of the Fool, within the happiness of daily life. We do not need to abandon the pleasures and satisfactions of success, at least not for now. Instead, we need to become aware of the center, the light shining behind and through the solid things of this world.

## DIVINATORY MEANINGS

In readings, the Six of Stones, like the hexagram, indicates great success and joy, but with the possibility that these things may not last. Other cards, such as the Ten of Stones, or the Universe, will give more solidity to the successes. Problem cards, such as the Five of Stones, would indicate danger ahead. Just as the Five of Stones might show a fear, so this card may indicate a hope. The person then needs to act to make the hope a reality. The Hagall pattern, and especially the hole in the center, urge the person to see the inner truth within the happiness. Use this success as a means to wisdom.

## REVERSED

Reversed, the Six of Stones shows the moment beginning to slide away. This does not mean disaster or certain failure. The other cards may indicate ways to use the current success to establish something more permanent. In financial terms the reversed Six of Stones would call for savings or careful investment while the money lasts. The person may have lost sight of spiritual values, seeing only the outer realities of wealth and not the light at the center.

## SEVEN OF STONES—FAILURE

The Tarot, like the *I Ching*, warns against extremities. From the success of the previous card we step down to failure. The elegant Hagall pattern of the stones falls back to the same sort of chaos we saw in the Five of Stones. Like a number of other problem cards, this one does not show only personal failure, though we might look at it that way for readings. The background of the card comes from *The Dying Unicorn*, the same painting used for the Four of Cups and the Five of Swords. It refers to the failure of a society that does not respect the Earth and the many forms of life that live upon it.

The hexagram is 12, titled "Standstill" (Stagnation) by Wilhelm, and "Stagnation" by Wing. The titles recall the meanings for the Universe reversed—not destruction but simply stagnation, a failure for things to develop to their full potential. The form of the hexagram is opposite to number 11, the hexagram on the Two of Swords. We see here the trigrams for Heaven above, and the Earth below. We might think that this shows the natural relationship between the two aspects. However, we need to remember that light lines naturally rise, while dark lines sink. Therefore, the tendency becomes for Sky and Earth, Spirit and matter, to separate.

Failure
Seven of Stones

Without a spiritual basis, material efforts fail. This idea seems alien in our culture. We think of business, for instance, as completely apart from religion. Business people may go to church, or try to behave ethically, or give to charity, but the actual work has nothing to do with the sacred. For archaic peoples, however, all acts carry a sacred dimension. If the divine awareness does not permeate our efforts, they fail.

The hexagram refers to the beginning of autumn, August-September, when the world experiences weakness within, harshness without. In social situations the inferior people have gained control. As in some of the Swords, the morally superior person had better withdraw from the situation than abandon moral principles.

In the picture the stones have lost any pattern. Human activity loses its meaning and purposes without that sacred connection. The stones are all different sizes, lacking balance and symmetry. The picture shows bare rock in the front, and behind, a sick tree bursting open. We see traces of blood on the rock and the nearly petrified wood. Despite these grim images the sky is clear, a sign of renewal.

## DIVINATORY MEANINGS

In readings we would tend to look first for some particular application. Does the Seven of Stones here refer to a project that has failed? The traditional meanings for the suit would suggest work or business. If the card seems to refer to a past experience, then the person needs to recover from it. Do the cards indicate the possibility of a fresh start? Or does the person still need to learn some lesson, or just allow time for strength and opportunity to return? If the card shows some future problem, the person can see it as a warning. Something is headed for failure and she or he must take a different approach. Perhaps some specific problem needs correcting. The person might look to see if some disharmony exists among the people involved. This meaning would become emphasized with some of the Swords cards, as well as Cups reversed. A wider possibility would be that the project lacks a spiritual dimension. The person needs to think why she or he is doing this, what she wants from the situation, or hopes to achieve.

More generally, and in connection with the hexagram, the card might show a general atmosphere around the person. (This would be the case if the card appeared in a position such as Environment or Other People.) The conditions are not good. If it refers to a job, the company may be badly run. Or maybe the people lack a sense of purpose or commitment.

## REVERSED

The reversed Seven of Stones would show a movement away from failure. If the failure has occurred in the past, then the reversed card shows a recovery or fresh start. If the position implies the future, it indicates that the person will avoid the collapse implied by the picture.

## EIGHT OF STONES—KNOWLEDGE

The title of the Eight of Stones does not mean simply a mass of information. It refers to what we might call "genuine" knowledge, that is, an awareness of the world which leads to understanding. Knowledge implies wisdom. The knowledge, therefore, is not just of techniques or research, but also of the way the world works, the kind of knowledge we get from studying the Tarot or the *I Ching*. Such knowledge can help us in business or romance or studying for a degree in a university.

Knowledge allows us to balance our efforts in the world. The seesaw qualities of the last few cards—success, failure, success, failure—comes under more control, so that the final three cards move steadily to solid achievement. The base for this movement is here in the Eight of Stones, in knowledge.

The hexagram is 62, which Wing calls "Prudence" and Wilhelm "Preponderance of the Small." This is similar to hexagram 28, which we saw on the Three of Cups. There we had four strong lines contained by only two weak ones. Here the weak lines are numerous. Strength and superiority must learn to direct the situation from within. This suggests moderation, a theme that joins with the idea of balancing the other cards. Wing says we must be conscientious about details. Both Wing and Wilhelm tell us to attempt small, rather than ambitious, projects. The hexagram resembles a bird, witih the two strong lines its body, and the others as the wings. A bird can soar very high but must return to the Earth. All these themes go well with the card and especially its place in the movement of the suit.

In this card we see order once again restored. The stones line up in a symmetrical pattern. However, a bubble forms the eighth stone. Thus we overcome the chaos of the Seven of Stones by understanding the need for the invisible in the company of the visible. In other words, our practical activities, and our knowledge of the world, require our opening to the "other world" of the Spirit.

The background of the Eight of Stones comes from Hermann Haindl's *Dream of India*. We see almost the same section of the painting as in the Six of Cups, with the temple pavilion and the soft light. The window carries the same meaning as the bubble, that of the physical world opening to something else. We saw a similar

Knowledge
Eight of Stones

theme in the open parts of the cathedral in the Two, Three and Four of Wands.

At the bottom we see a stone elephant. Because of their long life and slow movement, elephants symbolize wisdom and particularly ancient wisdom. The wise do not rush around. They do what needs to be done. The elephant symbolizes knowledge, the accumulation of wisdom which can be passed to later generations. In Indian mythology the God Ganesha, who wears the head of an elephant, is the patron of literature. According to some myths, Ganesha tore off one of his tusks to use as a pen, in order to write down the words of Valmiki, composer of the Mahabharata.

The elephant does not represent wisdom acquired by humans only. It also signifies the knowledge and wisdom of animals. The Native Americans do not view themselves as unique and superior to the rest of creation. Instead, they often refer to humanity as the "two-legged people" and the other animals as the "four-legged people." Plants, too, are conscious, as is even the very ground we walk on. As a figure of stone, the elephant signifies the wisdom of the Earth. To modern people, living in cities and coming from a largely intellectual religious tradition, the idea of the Earth as a conscious being, with Her own awareness and personality, seems almost impossible to grasp, let alone accept. Many people, however, see it as a fact of daily life.

## DIVINATORY MEANINGS

In readings this card signifies taking a careful and moderate approach to a situation. It calls for the person to acquire knowledge, to move slowly, with an eye to avoiding excessive action, either positive or negative. If the person has looked at things in a purely pragmatic way, the card suggests seeing the deeper meanings involved.

## REVERSED

Reversed, the Eight of Stones shows a lack of moderation. The person may be impatient, or taking too many risks. A literal reading of the title, Knowledge, would indicate ignorance, particularly if such ignorance brings danger. The person may be taking too narrow a view of the situation, refusing to recognize the bubble among the stones.

## NINE OF STONES—MATERIAL GAIN

A close look at the Nine of Stones will reveal the same background as the Four of Stones. The point of view has moved to the side and a little farther back. We see here the sky, the sea and the tail end of the mists, with only a glimpse of the great tree. There is more light here, with only a hint of darkness at the roots on the lower left.

The careful approach of the Eight of Stones has led to a more developed situation, with greater stability, than in the earlier cards.

**Material Gain**
Nine of Stones

Material gain is not an end in itself either for individuals or society. It is, however, a necessity, for without food and shelter people cannot even begin to pursue a spiritual path. While many Native American people practice ascetic denial during certain periods, such as a vision quest, the ideal of totally rejecting the world is as alien as excessive wealth. This comes from viewing the physical world as a sacred being.

The hexagram is 14, which Wing calls "Sovereignty" and Wilhelm titles "Possession In Great Measure." Success comes to the person through good fortune. Others find themselves drawn to the person and wish to follow her or his lead. We might expect such meanings to come from an image of one strong line among five weak ones. Instead, we see the opposite. The yang lines all flock to the yin because of the yin quality of modesty. The hexagram warns us that if we find ourselves in good fortune, we must continue a humble approach to life. This accords with the theme of the suit, where steady progress produces long-range stability.

We see two balanced lines of four stones each, with the ninth stone near the bottom, close to the Earth. The image suggests the Hanged Man. While this card depicts progress and gain, it rejects the idea of constant progress, constant economic growth. If a person or a society constantly seeks more and more wealth, they will never really use what they actually have. Good fortune can lead to bringing greater beauty and harmony into the world. Material success is a necessary first step for most people but still only a first step.

## DIVINATORY MEANINGS

In readings, the Nine of Stones indicates good fortune. It shows a likelihood of gain: more money, more security, better health, more comfortable conditions. If the Five of Stones should appear in the Past and the Nine of Stones in the Outcome, it signals great improvement. However, the person must avoid complacency, greed or conceit. The good things in the card may come from hard work, but they also come from a good "turn of the wheel." The person needs to recognize life's gifts.

## REVERSED

Reversed, the Nine of Stones does not indicate loss or bad luck so much as the danger of the person misusing the material gain. There is a possibility of greed, or more generally, the desire for more money and success than the person actually needs. It might be time for the person to step back slightly and look at goals.

# TEN OF STONES—RICHNESS

The stones in the Ten of Stones form the same pattern as the ten cups in the final Water card. This indicates to us that richness does not mean only material wealth (though it does not reject that either), but also happiness and a good life. In some decks this card represents mainly prosperity. Hermann Haindl has said that he

**Richness**
Ten of Stones

wanted this card to go beyond the traditional meaning in order to show the richness of an abundant nature, a sense of both the world and the individual person healthy and alive.

In the hexagram we find an image of the spiritual origins of wealth. The number is 48, which Wing calls "The Source." He describes it as the divine source of nourishment and meaning. Inexhaustible, it never changes, for it exists beyond the material forms it awakens. We can think of it perhaps as the light in the card of the Moon.

Wilhelm stresses the commonplace image that serves as the symbol, or inspiration, for this powerful understanding. He titles the hexagram "The Well," one of the two, along with "The Cauldron" (Three of Wands), that show a man-made object. In ancient China, styles of architecture varied greatly from region to region and in different historical periods. However, the wells remained the same design, everywhere and up to the modern age. Therefore, the well signifies something that does not change, whatever the location or outer circumstances. This gives the idea of an eternal truth. But since a well gives water, the most basic necessity of life, it also signifies the fundamental energy of being. Both Wilhelm and Wing stress that the hexagram teaches us to organize society around basic values and needs. Thus, in this mystical hexagram, we find a concern for justice in daily life.

The last of the Stones cards, the Ten of Stones shows the culmination of the pattern we've seen develop through the suit, and through the series of suits. Prudence and modesty have solidified the gains produced by good fortune, which in turn comes—as a response from life—after the person has acquired knowledge. And so we end with richness, where the stones in the Ten of Stones repeat the pattern of the Nine of Stones, except that the middle stone becomes doubled. This doubling indicates that the good fortune does not simply vanish, but establishes itself as a new basis for the person's life. And because the Stones cards are communal, these two stones go beyond the individual to society and nature.

The Ten of Stones can almost be said to culminate the entire Haindl Tarot as well. The Star and Aeon gave us images of the process of renewal. Here we look forward to the way the new world will be when the renewal has occurred. Knowledge and good fortune gain a wider meaning as well, because of this card. We can see them in the context of our planet's hope for "richness" or "health." The luck of Material Gain is the grace of protection we saw in the card Aeon, in Glastonbury Tor hidden among the mountains.

The background for the Ten of Stones comes from the *Oedipus* painting we saw with the Five of Wands. That card indicated conflict, and people striving to escape history. It also showed a personal transformation into the new. Here the transformation has been completed. In place of battle, we see new life. In a deep valley water rushes forth, white and foaming, like mountain snow melting in the spring. Above the cleft of rock we see a bright sky, brightest just above the middle stone, as if the sun is rising. The light appears vague, shining through a mist. We get a feeling that these remnants of clouds will soon vanish for already the sun is shining on the waters.

## DIVINATORY MEANINGS

In readings we once again bring the card down to the individual level. It should be clear, however, that the cards do not lose their wider implications when we interpret them in a mundane way. Part of the purpose of readings is to show the ways our lives mirror the patterns of the greater world. The Ten of Stones refers to a good life, to health and a sense of solid reality. Like the Universe, it shows the materialization of the person's hopes and desires. The meanings for the card may depend on the question. If someone asks about money then that is what the card will mean. But the other meanings will not vanish, even when we do not see them.

## REVERSED

Reversed, the Ten of Stones can have two meanings. One is that a potential good development has not yet occurred. This does not mean failure, but rather delay, as if the snow has not melted, or the sun has not risen above the rocks. Another meaning would indicate that the material wealth and security are there but the person does not appreciate their value. Too much attention has been focused on outer concerns without that inner dimension, that awareness of the Source, that gives Richness its meaning.

# MINOR ARCANA
# NUMBERED CARDS

| Number | Title | I Ching Hexagram | Wilhelm | Wing |
|---|---|---|---|---|
| Ace | | | | |
| 2 | Dominion | 26 | Taming Power of the Great | Potential Energy |
| 3 | Virtue | 50 | The Cauldron | Cosmic Order |
| 4 | Perfection | 63 | After Completion | After the End |
| 5 | Conflict | 49 | Revolution | Changing |
| 6 | Victory | 2 | The Receptive | Natural Response |
| 7 | Courage | 40 | Liberation | Deliverance |
| 8 | Swiftness | 35 | Progress | Progress |
| 9 | Power | 7 | Army | Collective Force |
| 10 | Oppression | 54 | Marrying Maiden | Subordinate |
| Ace | | | | |
| 2 | Love | 1 | The Creative | The Creative |
| 3 | Overflowing | 28 | Preponderance of the Great | Critical Mass |
| 4 | Mixed Happiness | 3 | Difficulties at the Beginning | — |
| 5 | Disappointment | 9 | Taming Power of the Small | Restraint |
| 6 | Happiness | 58 | Joyous, Lake | Encouragement |
| 7 | Illusions of Success | 4 | Youthful Folly | Inexperience |
| 8 | Failure | 41 | Decrease | Decline |
| 9 | Fortune | 42 | Increase | Benefit |
| 10 | Success | 46 | Pushing Upward | Advancement |

WANDS

CUPS

| | Number | Title | I Ching Hexagram | Wilhelm | Wing |
|---|---|---|---|---|---|
| **SWORDS** | Ace | | | | |
| | 2 | Peace | 11 | Peace | Prospering |
| | 3 | Mourning | 33 | Retreat | Retreat |
| | 4 | Truce | 24 | Return | Repeating |
| | 5 | Defeat | 47 | Oppression | Adversity |
| | 6 | Science | 61 | Inner Truth | Insight |
| | 7 | Uselessness | 36 | Darkening of the Light | Censorship |
| | 8 | Interference | 21 | Biting Through | Reform |
| | 9 | Cruelty | 6 | Conflict | — |
| | 10 | Ruin | 29 | The Abysmal | Danger |
| **STONES** | Ace | | | | |
| | 2 | Harmony | 16 | Enthusiasm | Harmony |
| | 3 | Work | 13 | Fellowship with Men | Community |
| | 4 | The Power of the Earth | 51 | The Arousing | Shocking |
| | 5 | Material Difficulty | 23 | Splitting Apart | Determination |
| | 6 | Success | 55 | Abundance | Zenith |
| | 7 | Failure | 12 | Standstill | Stagnation |
| | 8 | Knowledge | 62 | Preponderance of the Small | Prudence |
| | 9 | Material Gain | 14 | Possession in Great Measure | Sovereignty |
| | 10 | Richness | 48 | The Well | The Source |

# THE COURT CARDS

# INTRODUCTION
# TO THE MINOR ARCANA
# COURT CARDS

I N THESE SIXTEEN cards the Haindl Tarot moves the furthest from
Tarot tradition. As a European game (or esoteric system) from the
Renaissance, the Tarot uses the aristocratic structure to name its
people: King, Queen, Knight, Page. This pattern did not change until the twentieth century. The Golden Dawn and other esoteric
groups became dissatisfied with the imbalance between three male
images and one female. This did not stem from feminism, but from
ceremonial magic, which depends on a polarity of male and female.
Therefore, they created such designations as King, Queen, Prince,
Princess. Aleister Crowley used Knight, Queen, Prince, Princess.

Over the past ten or fifteen years people have sought to open
up the Tarot in various ways. Some feminists have created decks
based on women's spirituality. Other Tarot designers have created
pagan decks, or cultural decks, such as the Native American Tarot.
In many of these, the European Court cards become irrelevant,
leading the designers to choose their own figures. Some have re-
duced the Court cards to three per suit. This creates thirteen cards
(along with ace through ten), the number of lunar months in the
year. It also makes twelve Court cards, one for each sign of the zodiac.

When Hermann Haindl first thought about the Court cards for
his deck, he decided two things. He did not want the European ruling class, and he did want the traditional four in each suit. Next
came the decision to show each suit as a different culture. Partly he
was following the Native American idea of spiritual meaning in the
four directions. Each suit would signify a different direction. Together, they would show the various sacred traditions and approaches
to life around the world. As the center, Haindl chose an imaginary
point somewhere around the Mediterranean or the East Atlantic.
A European, he thought it right to view the direction from his own
position.

The attribution of the directions to the suits came partly from the symbols and partly from the elements. The suit of Cups belongs to the Holy Grail, a European object. This made Europe, which is North, Cups. On the other hand, Earth for Haindl represents the philosophy of Native America, while Fire for him signifies India. Therefore, West, America, becomes Stones, while East, India, becomes Wands.

As we saw the suits follow a particular order, determined by the elements: Wands-Fire, Cups-Water, Swords-Air, Stones-Earth. When we transfer these to the four directions we get the order Wands-East, Cups-North, Swords-South, Stones-West. This produces the pattern

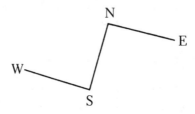

⌠ is a variation of the Eihwaz Rune found on the Star. Among other meanings, this Rune signifies the World Tree, which in turn unites the vertical directions of Above and Below with the Center and the horizontal directions.

The first time I met Hermann and Erica Haindl we talked about what names to give the Court cards. After some discussion Hermann decided on Mother, Father, Son and Daughter. This gives the cards a personal quality that balances the power of the mythological figures. It allowed Hermann to think of his own parents and children. The word "Court" for him reflects this intimacy. In most decks it means the royal court of King and Queen. But the word also refers to the central garden of a house, where a family might gather at the end of the day. When I went to Hofheim to visit the Haindls we sat in the court (the "hof" in German) and discussed the paintings.

Originally Haindl planned to use Israel for the South. Backed by Erica, I suggested that India and Israel were both East, and he might change the South to Africa. After some thought, he decided to make the South Egypt. This brought several advantages. Egypt represents an older culture than the Jewish or Christian. It clearly influenced both of them, as well as Greece. Also, Egyptian ideas and mythology have greatly influenced the esoteric interpretation of the Tarot. In many decks, Isis appears as the High Priestess, while some use Egyptian designs entirely. It therefore fits nicely to show Egyptian Goddesses and Gods, especially Isis, for one of the suits.

When Haindl thought about the different cultures he discovered a fascinating movement. India presents a long tradition, one that has ruled in its homeland for thousands of years. The Gods of ancient Egypt, on the other hand, lost their worshippers long ago, replaced by Islam. Yet, these figures are so compelling that their esoteric importance remains to this day. For Europe, Haindl chose the Grail legends, with Parsifal as the key figure. Here we see a one-time religious tradition that evolved into literature. We can guess at the Grail's sacred origins; we know of it, however, from a series of poems and stories. And finally, the Native Americans show us a sacred tradition, considered dead for many years, only to come back to life through the strength and courage of its people.

The change from Israel to Egypt brought a problem: no place to include Jesus Christ, or Moses. Haindl reconciled this for himself when he realized that Parsifal becomes a figure of Jesus (as we saw in the Fool), and that Odin suggests Moses, who received the Law as Odin received the Runes.

Hermann Haindl did not make his choices on philosophic grounds so much as a personal feeling for the different cultures. A European, he has spent time in both India and Israel, as well as America. In each place he felt a bond with the people and their traditions. When he changed the South to Egypt, he not only studied the mythology but actually traveled there, taking his paints and canvases with him.

For the images, Haindl has followed the different cultures. For India and Egypt he has used actual paintings of the various figures. Krishna and Radha, the Son and Daughter of Wands, came from posters that religious Indians display in their homes. The Cups cards came from a variety of sources. The Mother depicts a prehistoric statue found near the German town of Willendorf. For the Son and Daughter, Haindl created new images. For the Father, Odin, he returned to the mythological story shown in the Hanged Man, but followed the original version much more closely. With the West cards, he created his own pictures, using symbols, patterns and actual objects from tribal traditions.

The four directions contain different qualities but they all go together. The concept "North" means nothing without "South." All the suits follow a general pattern of development. The Mothers show us an ancient expression of the religion. Archaic and powerful, they go back to the basic energy. The Fathers take this energy and shape it into concepts. In Wands, for example, Kali represents a vision of the Absolute, the very source of existence. Brahma becomes more theological, concerned with advancing the culture. The four Daughters and Sons show the culture in its more human terms. Still mythological (except for the Son of Stones), they give us models of how people can act. Haindl has painted all the Daughters with a sense of love and calm. They show very different temperaments but each brings beauty and peace into the world. The Sons deal with the question of responsibility, again in different ways. The Sons of Cups and Stones form a polarity.

For the Divinatory meanings of those cards we "translate" the mythology into everyday terms. The usual "older man with blond hair and blue eyes" becomes irrelevant here. Instead, we need to look at what kinds of characters these people display. They can show us someone who delights in sensuality, like Krishna, or someone powerful but remote, like Odin.

We describe each card as a person. We say, "The Daughter of Stones is someone who. . . ." In fact, no one can be a Goddess or God. We can only be like them. And most people change their behavior and attitudes at different times in their lives. Therefore, these cards show us aspects of people. A Tarot reading describes a moment, even if it extends backward and forward in time.

In describing these cards and their meanings, I have relied on Haindl's statements about them plus my own limited knowledge of the cultures. For any mistakes, or any inadvertent insults to worshippers of some of these figures, I apologize in advance. The descriptions here are very brief. Some day, I expect, someone will write an entire book about these sixteen cards—their sacred and cultural origins, Hermann Haindl's use of them, the changes he has made in traditional representations, the relationships the cards form with each other and the lessons people today can learn from them. I look forward to reading it.

# WANDS—INDIA

FOR WANDS, Hermann Haindl has chosen the East, and for the East, India. (Specifically, he has chosen Hinduism. India is the home of other religions, including the Sikhs and the Jains. It is also a major center of Islam.) Haindl's choice is a personal one. Like many other people, he found his visit to India deeply inspirational. In India he found a land where religion and myth still play a vital role in daily life. For many people the sacred stories and hymns of Hinduism still possess divine power. Many myths end with the promise that whoever hears them will become healed of sickness.

It is not just the importance of religion in India that inspires people like Hermann Haindl. It is also the quality of that religion, its almost infinite variety, its staggering vastness of scale joined to the most human intimacy. In Christianity and Judaism, God created the universe some six thousand years ago. In Hinduism, the universe dances in and out of existence in cycles lasting 43,200,000 years. But this time is only a half-day for Brahma, the creator, who himself lives for 311,040,000,000,000 years and then will vanish, leaving only the ultimate Godhead. And yet, despite this vast scale, the Hindu deities are much closer, much more a part of daily life. We see them as lovers, tricksters, warriors, artists, yogis, dancers—and all the time we know that they, like us, only play out their roles in a magnificent panorama encompassing many worlds and many ages, but always moving toward that ultimate dissolution of the stage and all the players.

In India, Haindl developed a deep attachment to Krishna and Radha, his Son and Daughter of Wands. Not only did he experience the devotion they inspired in their birthplace, Vrindavan, he also came to admire what they represented. For Hermann Haindl this was a vision of the ideal man and woman as androgynous, sensual, delighting in life and art and sex. He loved their tricks, their individual freedom joined to devotion, their ability to switch roles, their sexual openness (one story tells how they made love while their friends watched and made comments). And he marveled that all this could occur in a context of sacred truth.

Though Haindl chose India for personal reasons, the choice was also logical. Wands is Fire, and Fire means the dawn, therefore East, therefore Asia. Fire and dawn also mean beginnings, and Hindu mythology goes back further than almost any living tradition. Moreover, Fire means inspiration, and Hindu myths and practices (such as yoga) have inspired religious traditions in many other places, including Europe, the Near East, China and Japan. Probably only shamanism reaches further back; and while much of Indian myth may reveal shamanic origins, the shamans of northern Asia show evidence of Indian influence.

Hermann Haindl considers Fire as magic (though magic more as a sacred power than someone doing tricks or manipulating nature). He identifies the Wand with the Magician and his transforming consciousness. The Magician wields a wand, but so do others. The conductor waves his baton, the teacher holds a pointer. All three direct, while combining different elements into a whole. Indian mythology consists, in fact, of many different mythologies, all of them bound together by a magical awareness. Haindl also identifies the Wand with the phallus, the lingam, that is, male generative power. This joins with the female power of the Earth. Fire is East and Earth is West, America, whose native people were also called Indians. Fire is the beginning of creation, Earth the result. We cannot hold or contain Fire, while the Earth is solid, materialized.

If India represents an ancient tradition, it also shows us religion and mythology as art. It comes to us as something ornate, removed from nature which it tends to disregard. Every gesture, every decoration, every dot of color, means something. Hermann Haindl told me that when he thinks of India, he thinks of magical tales, such as epics and wonder stories (including the *Arabian Nights*, many of whose plots may have come from India). Hinduism is also intellectual, as in the Vedas and the yoga sutras of Patanjali. All these things —magical stories, philosophy, art, sensuality—form a highly developed culture. The Haindl Court cards for Wands form a tribute to that culture and its sacred power.

## MOTHER OF WANDS—KALI

Kali Ma. The Black Mother, Mother Night. Kali Mahadeva. The Great Mother Goddess. The modern sage Sri Ramakrishna prayed

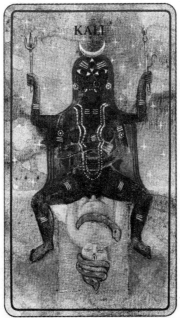

Mother of Wands in the East
Queen of Wands

for a vision before her statue. The temple, the floor, the walls, all disappeared. He knew nothing but the Mother. Later he wrote, "Maha-Kali, the Great Power, was one with Maha-Kala, the Absolute." European commentators and some Indians describe her as a "minor deity" or even a demon. For the people, however, Kali has always been important, even popular, despite her fearsomeness. She is Mother Kali.

For followers of Tantra, Kali is supreme. She is the Triple Goddess. She also is Creator, Preserver, Destroyer. Most people know these titles for the three primary Gods, Brahma, Vishnu, Shiva. But the Tantric texts insist that even Trimurti (as the three are called) were born out of Kali's infinite being. One of the keys to life—to accepting and rejoicing in the world—is the knowledge that the Goddess who creates the universe and the Goddess who destroys it are one and the same. Kali's main color is black, for non-being, the

Nothing beyond creation. But she also appears in red, for the Mother who gives birth, and even in white, for the pure Virgin. We see her here, as the Black Mother of Wands. She wears a Moon crown, like the High Priestess, the Tarot's own version of Absolute as female.

Kali epitomizes what Erich Neumann has termed "The Terrible Mother." We call her "Kali the Merciless," drinker of blood. Joseph Campbell tells us that until 1835 (when the British put an end to human sacrifice in India), priests beheaded a male child in front of Kali's statue in the city of Tanjore, at the temple of Shiva. The texts tell us that blood appeases her anger, and without it she will become uncontrollable, and destroy the universe. For Kali *is* Fire, and Fire destroys as well as creates.

For all the terror of her anger, Kali is not shunned by Hindus. Homes sometimes display shrines to Kali, for she protects her people against disasters. In one story, Kali first appeared (took shape out of her limitless being) when a great demon threatened the Gods. Even Shiva found himself powerless against the monster, and so Parvati (another aspect of Shiva's female side) knitted her brows and Kali sprang from her forehead. She killed the demon and then she went wild, dancing her ecstasy. Now, ecstasy is dangerous, the more powerful the more dangerous, for ecstasy breaks down the neat, orderly universe. With Kali threatening existence itself, Shiva went to plead with her. In her wildness she cast him down, and would have trampled him if some remnant of awareness hadn't broken through her dance, so that at the last moment Kali saw Shiva lying beneath her and forced herself to stop. But even though she ended her dance, she did not vanish back into Parvati. Once we experience that wild ecstasy, we can no longer pretend it does not exist.

The story of Kali dancing resembles very much a number of stories about Shiva, including a similar one where Brahma and the other Gods plead for his help in destroying a triple city of the demons. There, too, Shiva goes wild with excitement and begins a dance that will dissolve the universe. Shiva, too, stops at the last moment, with the promise that one day he will dance again and the universe will truly end.

We find roughly the same story about both Kali and Shiva because they *are* the same, two aspects of the divine energy that creates the magnificent illusion of the universe—with all its billions of stars, its unimaginable distances, its smaller and smaller molecules, particles, quarks—and will one day return it to Nothing. Shiva and Kali are the same, for like the Fool, they both come out of emptiness, and how can nothing be one thing or another? And yet—the great paradox—Kali is older, for she is Mother Night, and without her gifts life cannot exist.

Kali is the dark mirror of Shakti. We saw in the Empress how Shiva lies unmoving, like stone (a stone lingam) without the female energy to empower him. But if the Goddess can give the energy, she can draw it back. We see in the picture Kali copulating with a dead Shiva. Hermann Haindl has said that she has not killed Shiva, but that Shiva returns to her, gives himself to her. We see him upside down, like the Hanged Man. A snake winds around him, again in reversed form, for the tail begins over the crown, and the body coils past Shiva's third eye to wind around his chest.

We see Kali as black, with stars behind her and the Moon above her own third eye. When she destroys the universe, takes it back inside her, nothing will exist but the Great Night, the Deep, that which is truer and older than the separate forms of reality. She wears a red cloak, for Fire, and her red tongue hangs out, a symbol of life and strength. Erica Haindl refers to a similar gesture by Horus, the son of Isis and Osiris (Daughter and Son of Swords). Isis conceived Horus when she copulated with dead Osiris. Three lines appear in places along Kali's body. They signify the Triple Goddess. Notice that they form the I Ching trigram "Creative." And notice, too, that when the figure becomes doubled on her chest, it changes to the opposite trigram, "Receptive." The Great Mother contains all things.

Kali has six limbs, and six is the number of the Lovers. As we learned in the Major Arcana, spiritual ecstasy and sexual ecstasy arise from the same energy. Here we see the danger of that energy, even the reason why people suppress it. Kali's four limbs hold objects of her power. Since Haindl painted this card directly from traditional pictures, he himself has not identified the red mound before her belly. The other hands hold a three-pronged trident (also the weapon of Shiva) and a sickle. Though Shiva lies on a mat, Kali squats with her feet touching the Earth. She looms up huge against the sky; behind her we can see the curve of the planet.

The cards of East and South are culturally developed. Despite her ancient meaning, Kali appears stylized, with specific symbols and gestures brought together over centuries. The Mothers of North and West, by contrast, are more simple, direct. Yet behind Kali's artifice we see a living energy.

## DIVINATORY MEANINGS

In readings, the Mother of Wands signifies a person—not necessarily a woman—with a wild female kind of energy. She can be vindictive, even cruel. However, she can also be a loving mother. She exults in her own power. She does not recognize boundaries, especially those of conventional morality. She has a dark power and a wild sexual energy. As a lover she awakes and gives passion. Her partner, however, may feel overwhelmed at times, even frightened.

Hermann Haindl describes Kali as the strongest, the most magical of all the Mothers. He sees her as basically positive, for she represents a person who can deal with the dark energy of her own desires.

## REVERSED

Reversed, the Mother of Wands shows these things contained. A person has a Kali-like potential but stifles it, probably for the sake of being "nice" or "proper." The person might not even know she has this energy. Kali does not exist in the world until the Gods need her destructive power. And she springs full-grown from the forehead (like warrior Athena springing from the head of Zeus). This indicates that even though the power is sexual, it lies in the mind. With reversed Kali, the mind contains the energy, even hides it from conscious awareness. But if something triggers its release—the reading may concern that something—then it can overwhelm the person as well as those around her.

Another aspect of the reversed card would seem the opposite. It can indicate the destructive side of Kali taking over, outweighing the joy and love. The two aspects are related, for the powerful personality can become distorted when Kali tries to act in a conventional way.

## FATHER OF WANDS—BRAHMA

The Father of Wands is Brahma, the Creator in the Trimurti of Creator, Preserver, Destroyer. Despite the Tantra claims for Kali as the origin of all three, most Hindus see these as Brahma, Vishnu and Shiva. Western people tend to look upon this group as similar to the

BRAHMA

**Father of Wands in the East**
King of Wands

Christian trinity. However, while the Christian idea originates in a single Godhead, the three Hindu Gods are more loosely bound together. Hindu theology teaches that all Gods are manifestations of a single source. Historically, however, distinct sects (or religions) worshipped each of the Gods. We could say perhaps that while Christianity began as a single religion and later split into various Churches, Hinduism actually began as several religions that later became unified. Some rivalry remains, with some areas of India following one God (usually Vishnu or Shiva) more than the others. Just as Tantra claims that its primary deity, Kali, originated the others, so various stories describe Brahma, or Vishnu, or Shiva, as the source of all the Gods.

Brahma was originally the God of the priestly caste, the most intellectual and also the most patriarchal. He has never drawn the common people like the warmer Vishnu, or the wild Shiva. In the old myths the God Prajapati created the universe and the other Gods. The *Larousse Encyclopedia of Myth* describes Brahma as an abstraction of Prajapati, more of an idea. (We should not carry this too far. Brahma appears as an active character in many myths, much less of an idea than the Father in Christianity.)

The name possibly comes from Brahman, the holy power that gives life to the cosmos and everything in it. As Creator, Brahma would be the first manifestation of this power. We should not confuse him with the God of Genesis. YHVH is the unknowable source, while Brahma is the form the unknowable takes. Also, the creation in Genesis happens once and for all time. In Hindu myth, the universe lasts for a vast length of time, preserved by Vishnu at dangerous moments, until Shiva (or Kali) dissolves it in the dance. Then, after the long night, when only Brahma exists, creation once more emerges and the cycle begins again. As we saw in the introduction to Wands, Brahma, too, will finally vanish.

We see in the Father of Wands a traditional representation of Brahma. The footprint above his head comes from authentic symbology. It also links the Father of the East to Bigfoot, the Father of the West. Hermann Haindl has painted the picture in soft colors, giving us a sense of calm, of Brahma as balanced and unmoving. Joined to wild Kali, the picture conveys something of the androgynous quality of Hindu mythology. Like Kali he has four arms. The image suggests power beyond human limitations (how many times do people say, "I wish I had four hands"?). The number four also refers to universal law. We also see four faces. They symbolize the four elements, the four directions (important in India as in America), and the four yugas, the great ages in each cycle of creation. The four faces blend into each other. This reminds us that separateness is an illusion, a fascinating spectacle. Because the faces blend, they contain only five eyes. We also see five lines on Brahma's arms. In the Tarot this recalls the Hierophant, symbol of traditional wisdom.

Brahma wears a cord across his chest, a token of the priestly caste, or Brahmins. The white cloth signifies this as well, plus the fringed cape. Under the caste system each group wears different clothes, eats different foods, follows different restrictions, and so on.

The four hands show different aspects of the God. The upper-left makes a gesture, part of the complicated system of postures and body language that serves as prayer. The upper-right arm (the side of consciousness) holds a scroll containing religious laws (perhaps of the caste system, which so clearly favors the Brahmins). The lower-right hand holds a gold vessel, containing milk. The lower-left hand holds a spoon for stirring the milk in the holy fire. Milk is a sacred food in India, for cows embody the Goddess (Shiva rides on a bull). We see the same worship of the cow in Egypt and Scandinavia. In Norse myth the cow is the oldest creation. While in India, Erica Haindl attended a ceremony in which the priest offered milk and other foods as a sacrifice.

Brahma wears a decorated crown, signifying religion as a developed concept. In its various forms Hinduism stretches back thousands of years. Brahma takes the energy of Kali and calms it. As Creator, he channels it into existing forms. Kali is the night, Brahma the dawn.

## DIVINATORY MEANINGS

In readings Brahma signifies a man (or woman) who is calm, in command of the situation. He may tend toward passivity, or perhaps stuffiness. He follows traditional ways and expects others to do the same. At the same time he is without anger or aggressiveness. He possesses a rooted quality that gives strength to others.

## REVERSED

The negative side of the Father may come out in snobbishness, especially intellectual condescension to those less educated. He may believe too much in the "official" ideas of his society, dismissing as nonsense unorthodox concepts. On the other hand his attachment to tradition gives him a base from which to be kind to others. He does not just use tradition but believes in it. He is devout, not a hypocrite. As a father he loves his children, though they may feel a need to rebel against him.

Reversed, the Father of Wands becomes more down to Earth. He experiences doubts, weakness, confusion. If he comes through this experience he will emerge more tolerant of others, especially those who do not fit in with traditional patterns.

## DAUGHTER OF WANDS—RADHA

The Mothers and Fathers in the four suits signify the tradition itself. The Daughters and Sons bring the spiritual truths to the human level. They show us a personal expression of the values. Nowhere is this more true than in Wands. Krishna remains probably the most revered figure in Indian mythology. He and his wife Radha form the image of the perfect couple. They delight in love, in each other's bodies and minds. They show us love as playful and joyous. When Hermann Haindl visited India, especially Vrindavan, he found it a wonderful surprise to see a Goddess and God depicted in such a sensual way. The images seemed to him to create a genuine balance between male and female. They did not occupy distant poles, balancing each other in the manner of two equal weights. They mixed together, moved in and out of each other, each both strong and gentle, active and passive, devoted and playful. The myths depict them as changing clothes, even changing sex so that Krishna becomes Radha and Radha Krishna (an absolute taboo in Western tradition). At the same time it shocked Haindl to see how this marvelous balance did not seem to affect the actual behavior of the people, for Indian society puts women at a very low level, sadly remote from the image of Radha.

People in India sometimes refer to Vrindavan as still living in the Middle Ages. In a country where religion plays a great role, Vrindavan stands out as a center for devotion. As a vegetarian, Hermann Haindl must have found it a pleasant change to visit an entire city of vegetarians. According to him, people there look at food as medicine, for the soul as well as the body. Awareness of Spirit fills the air. When a friend of Haindl's brought him to the High Priest at the temple of Krishna and Radha, the priest said he had known they were coming. Krishna, he said, had told him.

Radha and Krishna are Gods, the incarnations of Lakshmi and Vishnu. But they are also human. In the cards we see them young and in love. They both hold flutes, the power of Wands translated into music. Radha's flute blends the colors of the rainbow, bringing the sensual joy of sight to that of sound. By playing, she pours her soul into the flute. The music gives soul to the material world. In Europe such figures as Plato and Pythagoras have taught of the cosmos as music.

Daughter of Wands in the East
Princess of Wands

The picture of Kali came from an old tradition. By contrast, the imagery in the Daughter and Son (taken from popular posters) comes from a nineteenth-century style of painting. Kali looked directly at us, confronting us with her fearsome truth. Brahma looks nowhere and everywhere, his energy diffused. But Radha and Krishna look gracefully to the side, at each other if we place the card of Radha on the left.

Radha wears a red dot on her forehead, a symbol of holiness but also of life. It matches the red of her lips. Above her forehead she wears three vertical stones; in the Tarot this recalls the Empress, who signifies sensuality, motherhood and wisdom. The stones are two green and one red. They symbolize life on both sides, for red represents the animal and green the vegetable.

Radha also wears a ring with a green stone. Though the detail comes from the original poster, Haindl based the ring on his grand-mother's wedding ring, which he had reset and given to Erica on the birth of their first son. Radha's green ring figures in a story that shows the playfulness of the lovers. Krishna steals Radha's ring. When she accuses him, he asks her why a simple ring should mat-ter so much. Radha waits for him to fall asleep and then sends her maidens to steal all his clothes. She then dresses as him and calls her-self Krishna. When Krishna wakes up naked he finds Radha's dis-carded clothes and puts them on. The anger gives way to pleasure as each one enjoys the sight of the other.

This and similar stories may have various meanings. We can say that they teach us to look at sex roles and even personal identity as nothing more than customs. This theme actually becomes a grand metaphor in the *Bhagavad Gita* (see Son of Wands). We might also consider that cross-dressing goes back to archaic practices of initi-ation. We find it as a sacred tradition among shamans in many tribal cultures. But what strikes us most about this story is its humor. The story does not lose its origins or sacred meaning, but gains an extra dimension of humanity.

## DIVINATORY MEANINGS

For readings Haindl describes the Daughter of Wands as a won-derful card, a sign of great abundance (the silks and jewels), but also joy. He describes Radha's jewelry and cosmetics as artificial but in a good sense, sign of a highly developed culture. This is a card of a happy person, someone gentle rather than passive, calm rather than weak. She is happy for she lives her life in beauty. Like the Son, the Daughter of Wands is sensual, she delights in sex. She is devoted to her partner, without losing her sense of herself.

## REVERSED

Reversed Daughter of Wands signifies someone repressing these qualities. Because of upbringing, fear or some oppressive situation, she does not allow herself to act out her sensuality, playfulness or self-confidence. The reversed card may indicate a person with a great potential that is not being fulfilled.

## SON OF WANDS—KRISHNA

The great epic, the *Mahabharata*, tells the story of Vishnu's incarnation as Krishna. In a central scene in that massive poem, Krishna tells the warrior Arjuna of the truth of the eternal soul. This passage, known as the *Bhagavad Gita*, has become a central text of Hindu belief, sometimes compared to Christ's Sermon on the Mount. Though the setting is a battle, its emphasis on duty and fulfillment helped inspire Mohandas Gandhi to develop the doctrine and practice of passive resistance.

Though Vishnu came to save the world he became fully human as Krishna. He provides Indian tradition with an image of the developed man. He is playful, lusty, a lover of tricks and music as well as women. These qualities, together with a childhood among the common people, have made Lord Krishna the most beloved of Hindu Gods. And yet, in the middle of his ordinary humanity he never loses his divine origins. One of the stories tells of Krishna's habit as a child of stealing food set out by the local women. When the women complained to Krishna's mother, she called him in and asked if he'd eaten any of the neighbors' food. He put on his most innocent face and told her he would never do such a thing—that she could look in his mouth and she'd see no trace of food. He opened his mouth. But when she looked in she saw the sky at night, the planets and the stars. The vision became vaster and vaster, and terror took her as she lost sight of the Earth, of herself, as the immensity swallowed her and she realized she was nothing. And then Krishna took pity on her and restored the illusion of her body, her home, her little son standing with his mouth open. She didn't see any bits of food, she told him, but she didn't want him causing any trouble. And she sent him out to play.

In this story we not only see the trickster Krishna, but also one of the great themes of Indian myth, the universe as a game in which even the Gods play their roles. In Krishna's speech to Arjuna the idea deepens to a profound message. Arjuna faces battle with his own cousin. How can he go on and fight, he asks his chariot driver—Krishna. How can he kill? Krishna tells him that the body does not matter. Only the soul is eternal, going on forever. As a warrior he must fulfill the duties of his caste. Whoever dies moves on to a new existence. For many people, sick of war and distrustful (at best) of all caste systems, Krishna's message seems wrong, for it tells

Son of Wands in the East
Prince of Wands

people to accept oppressive situations. The essential meaning, however, reaches beyond the circumstances of the story. Gandhi showed how we can use it to find strength for opposing war and colonialism.

Despite Krishna's service as a warrior, we see him more often as a lover of life. Many pictures show him surrounded by dancing women. Erica Haindl compares him to Dionysus, the Greek God of ecstasy. Krishna is feminine, a quality admired in Indian art. This androgynous ideal will startle many Western people. It belongs, however, in the Tarot, which teaches the merging of polarities.

In the picture we see Krishna in motion, playing his flute. This contrasts with Radha, whom we saw at rest. In traditional symbology the male represents action, the female stillness. We also see three-quarters of Krishna's body, in contrast to just the head and shoulder of Radha. This emphasizes sensual qualities for the male and mental for the female, a reversal of our usual view.

For both Krishna and Radha, we do not see the feet. Their bodies merge into the picture, which contains no objects or landscapes in the background. This gives them a dreamlike quality. Behind Krishna's head we see dark areas. The rest of the picture appears slightly stained and smudged. This evokes a subtle sense of the harsher aspects of the dream.

The poems always describe Krishna as dark and Radha as light. In pictures Krishna appears as blue, perhaps symbolizing the sky, or the sea. The blue halo behind him symbolizes the eye of a peacock feather, a symbol we saw in the Major Arcana cards Justice and Death. Krishna wears a red and green stone. These are the symbols Fire and Earth, as basic a polarity as Fire and Water.

Krishna plays the flute, bringing the divine music into physical reality. Like the Western Hermetic tradition, the culture of India recognizes five elements, which it links with the five senses. The fifth element is Quintessence, or Ether, and belongs to sound. Ether is the element of the Major Arcana, the "fifth suit." Some esoteric interpreters give a musical tone to each trump. The symbol for Quintessence is a dot. A dot signifies zero, or the Fool, the quintessential card of the entire Tarot.

In Vrindavan, Hermann and Erica Haindl attended a concert. Beforehand, the musicians gave an offering at an altar. Then the patron of the musicians gave them each flowers (like the chain around Krishna's neck). At the end of the concert some of the musicians gave their flowers as an offering to Krishna and Radha. Others, however, simply left them behind. This does not indicate rejecting the Gods but rather rejecting fixed rules. In this way offerings do not become automatic, without inner purpose. The Haindls also went to a play in which children portrayed Krishna and Radha. At the end, when the people applauded, it was clear they applauded the God and Goddess themselves.

## DIVINATORY MEANINGS

In readings Krishna means someone who loves life, especially its sensual sides. He has a great interest in the arts, and may be a performer of some kind. If not, he still looks at life as a performance, which he acts out with great style and elegance. He is a trickster, a lover of jokes. He can be serious, and is certainly loyal, especially to those closest to him. But even in his most dedicated moments, he will keep his sense of life as a game.

Sensual, physical, open, he attracts lovers. In a reading, if the card represents a (heterosexual) man, he genuinely loves women. He does not see sex as a means of proving himself, but rather as simple joy. If the card indicates a woman, she is very free sexually. The Krishna person will have many admirers, perhaps many partners, but he does not trifle with people. Others, however, may find it difficult to take him as he is. They may long to play Radha to his Krishna, even if someone else has taken the role.

## REVERSED

When we think of the Son of Wands reversed we may find it hard to imagine anything suppressing such a joyous personality. We can think of the reversed card as a testing. Some difficult situation, some unhappiness or conflict, requires the person to look at life more seriously. This may bring out unexpected depths in the person. Those who considered his love of play as shallowness may be surprised at his strength and single-mindedness.

# CUPS—EUROPE

W ANDS BECAME INDIA because of their connection with Fire, which suggested the dawn, and therefore East. The connection of Cups with Europe is more direct. The Cup is the Holy Grail. This makes Cups Europe, and since Europe is north of the other cultures, this makes Water the North. We can also see a connection with the rainy climate of northwestern Europe.

The Grail comes from Celtic culture, especially Ireland. Hermann Haindl has widened this to include his own Germanic culture. For the Mother he shows a famous statue found in Willendorf, Germany. He sets this, however, against a background of the Irish coast. The Father shows Odin, the German/Scandinavian God we saw in the Major Arcana. The Daughter is Brigid, from Ireland. Parsifal, the Son, is the only one directly connected to the Grail stories. However, the character of Parsifal derives less from Irish legend and more from French and German sources, especially a late medieval Grail epic by the German poet Wolfram von Eschenbach. Richard Wagner reworked this epic for his opera *Parsifal*.

Because they represented Haindl's own culture, the European cards became more ambivalent than the others. In dealing with outside traditions he felt it right to show what he admired of them, especially what he had found for himself. With Cups, however, he found it important to include the damage European culture had done to the world. This issue comes through especially in the Father and Son. The two cards also represent generational conflicts in present Germany, with Hermann Haindl (a grandfather) identifying with the sons.

The Cups show a vast sweep of history, from the Mother, a statue of thirty-thousand years ago, to a literary character found in contemporary books. This allows him to show the transformations of European culture. The most vital of these transformations is that from a religion based on nature to one based on theology and faith. The so-called Venus of Willendorf takes us back to early spirituality, with the Earth as Goddess. In Odin we find a patriarchal God but a pagan one. Odin indicates the pre-Christian period. Brigid

145

shows us the transition. A Triple Goddess of the Celts, she becomes taken over by the Christians, who made her a saint while keeping most of her pagan qualities. This single character, the Daughter of Cups, symbolizes that entire process by which the Christian religion absorbed the aspects of those old religions it did not destroy. Finally Parsifal—despite the story's pagan roots, we know it only in the Christian version. Parsifal as a character may be a late development, even if his type goes back to ancient initiations.

The transition includes a movement from the sacred to the secular. The Willendorf statue comes from an age when people experienced the sacred in all things, in the animals and tress and stone, in daily actions. Parsifal is a character in a story.

As we observed in the Major Arcana, Christianity is not native to Europe. It comes from a hot desert country. In the cold wet climate of Europe, it became more abstract, a religion of ideas. Possibly this has helped foster the European intellectual tradition. Other religions have moved beyond their original homes. In fact, the spread to other cultures forms a hallmark of theological religions. Buddhism spread to Tibet, China and Japan, while Islam spread over most of Asia, plus Indonesia, India and other places. The spread of Christianity, however, differs from these in two ways. First, it never really took hold in its homeland. Most Jews did not become Christians; later, Islam became dominant. Because it began within the Roman Empire, Christianity quickly moved away from its origins. Philosophically, Christianity owes as much to Greece as it does to Israel. In that way it parallels Buddhism, which took hold in China, Japan and Tibet, while becoming absorbed back into Hinduism at home, with the Buddha officially described as an avatar of Vishnu. The other factor is that Christianity supplanted the other religions of Europe. Even if some of their traditions survived through witchcraft (a controversial theory) they survived in such fragments, and so much on the outside of the official society, that most people today know nothing at all about them. By contrast, Buddhism coexists in Japan with Shinto and in China with Taoism and Confucianism. Islam rules much of black Africa but not all of it. It coexists not only with Christianity but with Animism, a loose term to describe the various native traditions.

Of the four Cups Court cards, the Mother, Father and Daughter all show the land. When we come to Parsifal he has separated from nature, and even from his own body. We see only the head and hands. His amazed stare at the Grail represents, among other things, his rediscovery of nature. We see water in both the Mother and Daughter. Odin must reach into the well of Mimir to retrieve the Runes. Parsifal, however, still struggles with the question of whether to raise the cup to his lips and drink. To drink from the Grail means surrendering himself to something greater than his own desires.

The Grail is very old. For Hermann Haindl it signifies all humanity, for he thinks of it as coming from Atlantis. At the same time, it symbolizes Europe's particular contributions and values. We might identify these as emotion, love, a concern for humanity and especially the oppressed. The Grail also indicates the European idea of the individual. The Goddess of Willendorf shows the sacred as something abstract—the idea of the female, without even a face. When Parsifal holds the Grail before him, with its light flooding his face, he alone must meet the challenge.

## MOTHER OF CUPS— VENUS OF WILLENDORF

The title of this card refers to the statue shown in the picture. Willendorf is the place where archaeologists unearthed that ancient carving, created some twenty-five to thirty thousand years ago. The term "Venus" comes from a habit of referring to all prehistoric female figures as Venus. In a sense, this custom goes back to the Roman Empire, whose people tended to identify any Goddesses of other cultures as variations of their own. Archaeologists also use this term because of an assumption that any female image must refer to a "fertility cult," a term that belittles not only female-centered religion, but also the consciousness of prehistoric peoples. The last habit is very deeply ingrained in our culture. We find it difficult not to think of humanity as more and more "primitive" the further back we go. In fact, the more research we do into stone circles and ancient temples, the more we discover their builders' sophistication in such areas as engineering and astronomy. And the more we try to understand the archaic view of the world, the more we see it as a subtle and complex recognition of nature, sacred reality and human psychology. We might better call this statue the Great Goddess of Willendorf.

This does not mean the statue does not symbolize fertility.

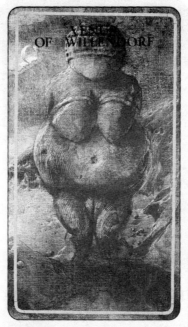

**Mother of Cups in the North**
Queen of Cups

Clearly the pendulous breasts, the round belly and hips and the sturdiness show her as an idea of motherhood. The problem comes from a view of female fecundity as somehow of minor importance, not the subject of true religion, which we think of as intellectual, apart from nature, "in the sky"—and masculine. Some people will view this figure as odd-looking, even ugly or funny. We have learned to see the ideal female as thin and weightless, unconnected to such distasteful realities as childbearing or work. Such attitudes distort our perceptions of beauty.

Of all the Court cards, only the Mother of Cups derives from an object rather than a painting or a mythology. Because of the statue's age we know little about it. We can guess but we should do so with the recognition that we base those guesses on assumptions. And yet, we need to make connections to such figures because they belong to our origins. Statues and cave painting tell us several things. First, they demonstrate that spiritual awareness goes back to the beginnings of human culture. Evidence indicates that when humans first learned to control fire, they used it for religious ceremonies rather than warmth or cooking. Secondly, the figures display a sophisticated artistic sense that shows art as basic to human nature.

Ancient statues and drawings usually lack faces. This may indicate a lack of individuality, or a sense that sacred reality transcends personal qualities. This reality begins in stone. Lucy Lippard, a writer on the links between prehistoric and contemporary art, has pointed out the sacredness of stone. Cave entrances served as holy sites. Closer to modern times people have built temples to align with mountains shaped like breasts. In many cultures, mining and metalworking have been sacred acts, performed in secret by special orders (compare this to Freemasonry, which began as an esoteric order). If we see the Earth as Mother, then mineral deposits become embryos in Her womb. And rocks or pebbles, or simply markings shaped like a woman, or the Moon, become objects of worship. The next step might have been for people to make their own forms, painted on rock walls, or shaped from a lump of stone. From all the evidence, art began as a way of joining consciousness to the divine.

In this Tarot card we see some of these themes. Behind the statue, on the right, lie rocks in the shape of balls. On the left we see the idea of a ball, one of Hermann Haindl's spiritual bubbles. The two together could symbolize that great leap when humanity discovered the abstract conception within the concrete reality. The original statue does not have feet. Haindl has painted the legs going into the ground. She does not walk the Earth so much as grow out of it. She *is* the Earth. We also see the Goddess's connection with the Moon, shown on the upper left, and the sea, for he has placed her against a background of a beach.

According to some commentators, the stripes over the breasts represent arms. They may also indicate snakes. The circles of holes on the head have evoked various guesses. They form a spiral or labyrinth. Hermann Haindl thinks of them as hair, while Erica Haindl has suggested they might have held feathers or else opened the head to energy pouring down from the sky. In India the third eye (which some people identify with the pineal gland behind the forehead) opens to awareness of divine light. Might earlier people have seen the whole head in this way?

The presence of a landscape marks a change from the Wands

cards, where culture had supplanted nature. The card moves the statue to Ireland. Just as the Mother shows a German statue in Ireland, the Son shows a figure from a Celtic myth (originally Irish) which became a literary work in Germany.

The landscape is green and fertile, though without trees. When the Haindls visited Ireland they found few trees. In many places the people had cut the trees down long ago. The coast may never have had trees due to the rough sea and wind. The land appears gold in the foreground of the card as if it basks in the light of the Cup. A diagonal line runs from the Cup to the Moon, while another runs from the sea up the line of hills, echoing the Hanged Man. The Moon is a crescent, with a darker area at the bottom. This recalls the High Priestess. The Moon shines through a hole in the dark clouds. The belly of the Goddess, like the ball before the High Priestess, signifies the full Moon.

## DIVINATORY MEANINGS

In readings, the Mother of Cups signifies someone very earthy, someone plain and honest. She is creative and imaginative, but does not lose her connection to the basic realities of life. The card may signify a mother, one devoted to her children, possibly a matriarch to whom the whole family looks for support.

As an abstraction, not depicting a particular person, the card signifies a sense of ancient forces, an awareness of nature and spiritual energy filling the ordinary things of daily life.

## REVERSED

Reversed, the Mother of Cups can show someone out of touch with the physical realities so important to her. It may be the situation of a mother whose children have grown up and left home, or of a person with great energy and no valuable place to put it.

## FATHER OF CUPS—ODIN

For the Father of the North, the Haindl Tarot returns to All-Father Odin, who figured so importantly in the Major Arcana.

**Father of Cups in the North**
King of Cups

There we saw Hermann Haindl's reworked version of the myth, with Odin first as the arrogant young Emperor, and then as the joyous Hanged Man, returning his energy to the Earth. Here we see the original of the scene from the Hanged Man: one-eyed Odin hanging on the World Tree for nine days and nights, "myself sacrificed to myself," in order to bring up the Runes from the dark well of Mimir. With the Hanged Man, Haindl followed his intuition, painting the picture as he received it. Here in the Father of Cups, he stays with the sources, especially the Elder Edda. No ancient pictures of Odin have come down to us; Haindl relied instead on the poems. He has commented that if he'd created the picture entirely from his own imagination, he might have painted only one eye, in the middle, like a Cyclops. However, the myth makes it clear that Odin had two ordinary eyes and gave one as an offering to Mimir.

In the card we see the left eye is missing. The left is the side of the unconscious. Odin joins his own unconscious side to the greater mystery of Mimir's well, the dark source of life. Remember the *I Ching* hexagram 48, described as "The Well" by Wilhelm and the "The Source" by Wing. A certain scientific theory of creation holds that the overwhelming energy which coalesced into our universe originally poured out of a "white hole," that is, a black hole in another universe.

The right eye is consciousness. By finding the Runes, an alphabet, Odin moves humanity from the dream of myth into the hard reality of literal thought. Erica Haindl comments that this card shows the beginnings of linear history, of technology, of the world broken into pieces. For it shows the invention of writing, which puts knowledge outside the person.

Odin signifies power, the most powerful of the Fathers, a partner to Kali. As both Sky-Father and God of the Underworld, he wields the power of life and death. He is creator, thinker, warrior, prophet, the various faculties seen as important in Western culture. But Cups represent love and peace. Therefore, the card implies a tension. Odin shows the dominance of power, the right eye. Later, Parsifal (both eyes staring) will confront the same tension in himself, the battle between power and love.

The suit of Cups is emotional. The masculine ideal considers emotion weak. But Odin is very emotional. Hermann Haindl has observed that aggression comes out of emotion. In the picture we see the first finger pointing. Haindl describes this gesture as the "aggressive love" of the Father. The finger represents the virile phallus—the lingam of Shiva without the yoni of Parvati. Remember that the Goddess of Willendorf comes from a much older period than Odin, and that Odin's religion of the Aesir replaced the more peaceful Vanir, who worshipped the Mother. Palmists refer to that first finger as the "Jupiter" finger, connecting it to the All-Father of the Romans.

For Haindl, Odin symbolizes the qualities he finds difficult in Europe and especially Germany. He sees Odin as aggressive, conquering. At the same time he clearly admires Odin as the shaman, the Oracle, the Father of wisdom. He has suggested that perhaps his own experiences of the sometimes-difficult relationship between a son and a father have come into this card.

We have seen elsewhere how Odin had to hang upside down in order to pick up the Runes. The Runes come from the Earth. Compare this to Moses, who gets the law from the Sky and then engraves it on stone. Jesus rose head first when he went up to Heaven. Odin goes head first down to the well. His hair and beard radiate like the Sun, so that light surrenders to darkness in order to bring out knowledge.

As the Emperor, Odin acknowledges only himself. But he can only gain the Runes by hanging on the World Tree. The tree here has a double trunk, symbolizing duality. We also see the two birds, Thought and Memory. Haindl based the tree on the olive trees around his house in Tuscany. These very often have holes at the bottom. The southern trees with the northern God mix together the cultures of Europe. We also see a cypress tree at the back. Like the ravens, the cypress signifies death. Like Jesus, or maybe upside-down Peter, Odin presents a drama of death transformed. He appears bigger than the tree, an indication that in this card, thought dominates nature.

The Runes spell TAROT. They include the O Rune, Othal. As we saw in the Major Arcana, Zoltan Szabo links this Rune with the Holy Grail.

## DIVINATORY MEANINGS

In readings the Father of Cups signifies a powerful, domineering kind of person. He (or she) is intelligent, creative, likely to know a great deal. He can be very intimidating, especially to his own children. He can also be generous and loving, as long as those around him recognize him as patriarch. He may be a magician, perhaps an artist of some kind. For a full portrait of the actual person we need to look at the cards around the Father of Cups. Gentle cards, especially other Cups, will bring out the love in the Father. More arrogant cards, such as some of the Wands or Swords, will emphasize his domineering quality. The Magician or the Chariot will develop the magical side.

## REVERSED

Reversed, the Father of Cups shows the Father's power disrupted in some way. He no longer rules unchallenged. Others may push him, or else he faces a situation beyond his control. This can bring various reactions. He may turn nasty, but he also may show more compassion. The other cards should give a hint of which direction he is likely to go.

## DAUGHTER OF CUPS—BRIGID OF IRELAND

Hermann Haindl painted the Court cards last, for it took time before he knew how he wanted to do them. When he had decided on using the four compass directions but had not yet begun, he visited America. There he discussed the different possibilities with a Native American friend. The man told him of Bigfoot, who then became Father of Stones. He also said that Haindl should have the Daughter of Cups be Brigid. Though Haindl knew very little about this figure, he decided to follow the suggestion. He painted a face based on that of his wife and set her in a landscape indicating ancient European spirituality: a ring of standing stones, and a river leading to a cave.

The choice has turned out to be a valuable one. Haindl knew of Brigid only as an early nun who became a saint. In Ireland she ranks almost with St. Patrick himself. In fact, the story of Brigid goes back much further than Christianity. Called Bride in Scotland and Brigantia in England, she was a Goddess of the Celts. Brigid was Goddess of poetry, prophecy and divination, a perfect figure for the Tarot. She had two sisters, also named Brigid, one a patron of healing, the other of smithery (in the Mother of Cups we saw the sacredness of metalworking). The three were probably one, a version of the Triple Goddess. In fact, the name Brigid originally meant Goddess. Literally, the word means "exalted one."

When Ireland became Christian, Brigid became a saint. Little else about her changed. If anything, her importance increased, for as well as receiving the worship of poets, she became patron of livestock and produce. Her feast day, February first, was originally the beginning of Spring. St. Brigid was born at sunrise, neither within or without a house—that is, on the threshold. In Celtic tradition, moments or places that are not one thing or another—as dawn is neither day or night—open the way to the Other World. The stories tell us that Brigid fed on the milk of a white cow with red ears. The colors indicate a supernatural origin. As in Scandinavia and India, the Irish looked on cows as sacred. When St. Brigid stayed in a home, she gave off such light the house appeared to be

Daughter of Cups in the North
Princess of Cups

on fire. We read of Zoroaster that even in the womb he gave off such light the neighbors rushed to put out the fire. Giraldus Cambrensis tells us that Brigid and nineteen other nuns took turns guarding a sacred fire. The fire was surrounded by hedges that no man might enter. In Roman Britain, the sanctuary of the Goddess Minerva, forbidden to men, contained a perpetual flame. We might also think of Sleeping Beauty, whose castle was sealed off from the outside by magical thornbushes.

Brigid demonstrates the carryover from pagan religion to Christianity. In ancient Ireland three classes of poet/priests ruled alongside the kings. These were the Druids, the Filidh and the Bards. When the country became Christian the Druids were banned, but the Filidh inherited many of their powers and functions. The Filidh worshipped Brigid. In the movement of the Cups cards from a long-lost religion of the Earth to modern Christianity, Brigid fits very well between Odin and Parsifal.

The card contains a kind of history of the sacred in Europe. The cave shows the earliest form of temple. The stone circle gives us the beginnings of human creations mimicking natural formation. We see as well the face of the Goddess and the sacred cup of the Holy Grail, a Christian symbol. The rolling hills form layers, like the layers of history and myth. We see her behind the hills. She is the origin of all mythologies and religions. The hills form her dress, or her body, with the cave going into her mysteries.

The stones do not depict any particular stone circle, but rather the idea. They form lingams but the circle is a yoni, while the cave and the river belong to the Goddess. We see six stones. In the Tarot six stands for the union of male and female in love. We find the same union implied in the pink color at the base of the stones and the blue of the river and Brigid's eyes.

## DIVINATORY MEANINGS

In readings the Daughter of Stones shows a person with a calm but radiant quality. She may seem withdrawn to others, certainly less exuberant than her cousin the Daughter of Wands. Many people, however, will find themselves drawn to her peacefulness and strength of character. Around her, other people gain a sense of their own depths, their own possibilities. As a principle, the card signifies poetry and divination. Originally people did not make a separation between poetry and sacred truth. Odin used the power of magic. Brigid suggests the source of that power, like the Shakti of Shiva. She gives us a glimpse into the ancient caves. Odin was written history. Brigid takes us back to the stone circles.

## REVERSED

The Daughter of Stones reversed indicates a person who has lost her calm self-assurance. Something—troubles, pressure from others —has moved her away from her center. She may need to get back her own awareness of herself before she can take any positive action. The Daughter of Cups indicates the importance of personal history. If she knows her origins and her own strength, nothing can shake her. This becomes especially true if the card appears, right side up, with Strength, or the Star, or the Four of Stones. Reversed indicates that she has lost this basic truth. Nevertheless it still exists. The person may need to explore her past in order to build up trust in herself.

## SON OF CUPS—PARSIFAL

From the most ancient card, the Goddess of Willendorf (Mother of Cups), we come to the most modern, Parsifal, a character rather than a religious figure. The Grail story carries us from the ancient Celts to now, for along with the medieval romances and Wagner's opera we have T. S. Eliot's poem *The Wasteland,* plus various novels such as the recent ones of Richard Monaco, and John Boorman's film *Excalibur,* in which Parsifal also becomes the Hanged Man, for he discovers the Grail while hanging from a tree.

In the Haindl Tarot as well, Parsifal discovers the Grail. We see him staring at it with astonishment, even shock, as the light fills his face. Now, this moment carries different symbolic truths. On the one side it signifies the discovery of spiritual truth, something greater and deeper than personal desire. Parsifal was a normal young man (if excessively naive), with an ambition to become a knight and serve King Arthur, like the other heroes of his time. And then he confronts the Grail—he is forced to confront the Grail. He becomes aware of divine truth, and the presence of the Holy Spirit. This challenges him to goals beyond his own gratification.

But we can look at Parsifal's shock as another kind of discovery —the terrible things done to the world by the "Father," that is, previous generations. In many places, young people (and others who identify themselves with the future) have been confronting the damage done to nature, the dangers of arms races based more on greed than defense, and the ideologies of conquest, empire and genocide. Hermann Haindl sees Europe today as finally beginning to recognize what it has done to the rest of the world. No wonder Parsifal appears shocked, even terrified. He does not face only the past but the future: that is, his own responsibility, as Son of the North, to fulfill the Grail quest. In contemporary terms this means helping to restore the Earth, and set his people back on a spiritual path.

We saw in the Fool how Parsifal killed a swan. This came from his desire to use weapons like a genuine knight. Other creatures

Son of Cups in the North
Prince of Cups

were not real to him. This mirrors the mentality of colonialism and slavery as well as those who destroy nature for profit. But Parsifal's action caused him to discover sin, and death, and finally responsibility. In the card he appears like a modern European student, with his long hair, uncombed and blown to the side. We see him compelled to take up the Grail.

In various ways problems of exploitation and racism exist throughout the world. Hermann Haindl has concentrated these questions on Europe for two reasons. One, he is a European. Second, he feels deeply the impact Europe has had on the rest of the world. Geographically, Europe does not even exist. It forms a corner of Asia. And yet in a variety of ways it has conquered or disrupted at different times Africa, America, Australia, Oceania and much of Asia. Whole peoples have been wiped out of existence by a culture that thinks of itself as following a God of love. When we discussed this card Hermann and Erica Haindl told me of a friend's reaction to the "Turkish problem" in Germany. A Native American teacher, their friend had heard about Turkish immigrants supposedly disturbing German society. She proposed a solution: Germany could send all its foreigners to America, and the Native Americans would send back all *their* foreigners to Europe.

In the Son of Cups we see Parsifal as he takes up the challenge, rather than in fulfillment. In contrast to the Hanged Man, or his sister, the Daughter of Cups, he appears detached from nature. Her eyes looked up from the hills, his look down, seeing only the Grail. His hands appear like clouds, or x-rays. They also become the hands of Spirits giving him the Grail, which he must take. His mouth remains closed, like the Fool. This indicates ignorance, but also a reluctance to take up the challenge. In the story, the first time Parsifal encounters the Grail he fails to ask the key question, "Whom does the Grail serve?" He must learn to serve, he must recognize the wasteland as his own responsibility.

In designing the Court cards, Hermann Haindl faced the issue of where to put Jesus. He solved the problem when he realized that Jesus lives within Parsifal. Jesus here is a man rather than a God. He, too, had to face the moment when he took up his true work. For years he had lived the life of a carpenter. Parsifal shows Jesus waking up to the divine reality that will lead to his own crucifixion.

## DIVINATORY MEANINGS

In readings the Son of Cups shows someone who is sweet-tempered, though naive. He may appear to others as self-centered or callous, but this comes primarily from a lack of experience. Possibly his parents have sheltered him too much and always given him everything he wants, so that he does not know what it means to suffer. Other people's troubles do not touch him because he does not compare them to anything in his own experience. Underneath, however, he has a good heart. Even if he acts selfishly, his real basis is love. He himself may need to discover just what love means. He can be very open, good-natured. He likes to see people happy. If they become unhappy or show themselves in pain, he may want to run away.

More than the other cards, the Son of Cups indicates a moment as well as a personality. This shows him being tested. He faces the knowledge of suffering, as well as his own responsibility to do something about it. This can lead to greater self-knowledge as well as a greater sympathy with others.

## REVERSED

Reversed, the Son of Cups indicates the person trying to avoid responsibility. It shows Parsifal refusing the Grail. We may see him as someone bitter or disillusioned because the world turns out less pleasant than he's always believed. He may feel overwhelmed by others' suffering. His callousness may become more extreme as he avoids his own stirrings of love.

# SWORDS—EGYPT

AS DESCRIBED IN THE introduction, Hermann Haindl first planned to use Israel for the direction South. The change to Egypt came partly through the realization that South, for Europe, means Africa. Europeans tend to think of Egypt as a European culture, and in fact, much that is characteristically European comes from Egypt via Greece and Israel. But Egypt also belongs very much to Africa.

Haindl knew India and America personally, but not Egypt. After reading of the mythology and the ideas, and deciding which figures he would use for his cards, he then went to Egypt to experience the people and the land. The paintings were done in Egypt itself, using the light and the colors, as well as examples from temples and tombs. As a result, the Southern cards have a vivid and deeply felt immediacy.

Not using Israel worried Haindl because it meant none of the cards would show Christ. He resolved this partly by realizing that Parsifal, the Son of Cups, symbolizes Jesus. When we look into Egyptian religion, especially the figure of Osiris, we discover that this very ancient religion points directly to Christianity.

We also find many parallels to Indian myth. Again we see an ancient Goddess associated with the night. We also find a somewhat remote creator, the God of the priestly and royal levels of society. Like Brahma, Ra took over from earlier figures. Eventually, they became part of him, so that Atum changes to Atum-Ra. And as with Brahma, so Ra's followers maintained that he emerged out of nothing. Whereas some earlier texts described Nut as his mother, later versions refer to her as Ra's granddaughter. Finally, just as the ordinary people revere Krishna, the ordinary people in ancient Egypt worshipped Osiris as a beloved savior.

Like Indian mythology, the Egyptian stories are very complicated, and for similar reasons. Originally, each region had its own Gods. When they merged, different characters fulfilled different functions at different times. Nut changes generations. Thoth and Hathor are minor figures in some versions, major in others. Isis took on various qualities of Nut and Hathor, while Osiris changed from a vegetation God to a lord of the afterlife.

Certain features, or motifs, remain constant. The Sun, as a red disk, appears in many myths and paintings, primarily of Ra, but also for Isis and others. In a desert land like Egypt, the Sun plays an ambivalent role, the giver of life energy, but also the burning eye that stares down mercilessly. Throughout Egyptian mythology we find the motif of the eye. To crush a rebellion, Ra gives his eye to Hathor, who uses it to kill the disobedient humans. Horus's eye brings revelation. The picture Haindl chose as his model for Osiris displays two ornate eyes, one on either side of the God.

Unlike most cultures, the Egyptians saw the Sky as female, the Earth as male. Nut symbolizes the arching night sky, in intercourse with her brother Geb, the Earth, whose phallus is the obelisk. But the obelisk also symbolized Ra, for it contains the creator's masculine power. Hathor also formed the sky, though she lost much of her influence to Nut and Isis.

Unlike Indian religion, the faith of ancient Egypt lost its believers many centuries ago. Yet its influence remains. In the ancient world, in such places as Greece and Israel, Egypt became known for magic, esoteric truth, and initiation. Mystery religions in ancient Rome based themselves on Egyptian myth. The fascination of the pyramids, the hieroglyph picture-writing and the complex treatment of the dead helped to maintain this reputation. So did detailed texts such as the Books of the Dead. A myth developed of Egypt, and this myth still flourishes. Books appear on the secrets of the pyramids, occultists describe the Egyptians as the heirs of Atlantis. These claims may be true or not. The *image* of Egypt has dominated hermetic tradition for many centuries.

The myth of Egypt has greatly affected the Tarot. Court de Gebelin first announced that the Tarot was the Book of Thoth, the secret text of universal knowledge. Later decks depicted the High Priestess as Isis, an idea helped along by Madame Blavatsky's identification of Isis with her own doctrines (derived partly from India). Many Tarot decks contain Egyptian figures on the Wheel of Fortune, and many commentators identify the card with Ma'at, the Egyptian idea of universal order. Ma'at was maintained by Hathor, Goddess of love and the law of life, which has given rise to the famous sentence, "Rota Taro Orat Tora Ator." The Wheel of Tarot Speaks the Law of Life.

We saw in the Major Arcana how the esoteric Tarot identifies the Magician with Thoth whom it further links with Hermes, the

Greek God of wisdom. Thoth is an extremely interesting figure. In Memphis, where people worshipped Ptah, the God of life energy, Thoth acted as Ptah's agent, and as the God of the Moon and of wisdom. In other places and times he became Horus's agent or Osiris's scribe. Thoth invented writing as well as magic, and taught both to his disciples. When Ra forbade Nut to bear any children on any of the days of the year, Thoth gambled with the Moon to gain five extra days, thereby allowing Isis and Osiris to be born. In one story of Ra we learn that Ra retired, and gave the rulership of the world to Thoth.

In all these myths Thoth appears as a helper. In the central myth of Ra, Nut, Isis and Osiris, Thoth is the outsider, the only important figure not a member of the family. This fits a particular occult ideal, that of the figure in the background, secretly shaping history. Perhaps Thoth was a very ancient deity, displaced by later religions but never completely forgotten. Or maybe Thoth, like Odin, was an actual person, a shaman, whose knowledge and mastery of magic raised him to the level of a God.

Thoth forms an ideal figure for the patron of Tarot and especially the suit of Swords, even if he himself does not appear in the four cards. He represents mind, esoteric truth and the use of power in the service of wisdom.

## MOTHER OF SWORDS—NUT

Most people know Nut (sometimes called "Mother of the Nine") as the night sky, arched over the Earth, her body filled with stars. She appears very slim, almost a ribbon in some pictures, with the suggestion that she reaches all about the Earth. Hermann Haindl has based his image on temples in Dendera and Edfu, and the ceiling of the tomb chamber of Ramses VI. The image is very ancient, for Nut, like Kali in India, goes back to primordial times, with her Libyan version, Neith, described by Vicki Noble as possibly "the oldest Goddess in the world."

Some images show Nut in intercourse with her brother Geb, the Earth, who appears lying on his back with Nut arched over him (the opposite of the "missionary position" by which the Christian Church dictated that the man must always be on top). The obelisk symbolized Geb's penis as well as the power of Ra. The scene makes Egypt

Mother of Swords in the South
Queen of Swords

one of the few cultures to picture the Sky as female and the Earth as male. But Nut is the night sky, maintaining the idea of the day—the light as male (Ra, the Sun), and the dark—the ancient and mysterious as female.

Nut sometimes appears standing upright on her toes, as shown here in the version behind the arching woman. In fact, the two images are the same, for the upright posture represented Nut seen from beneath. It appears on the inside of coffins (Haindl saw this in Medinet Habu and on a coffin in the Egyptian Museum in Cairo). Nut reaches over the dead person who would "see" her from beneath, in contrast to her profile in the Sky. Night and death become alike in this double-image of the Goddess. Death covers us entirely, the way the night covers the Earth. While Mother Nut confronts us with the fear of darkness, she also shelters us. Her presence in the coffin would help to assure the passage of the soul through the chaos of death to the order of a new life in the Other World. Just as the Sun is reborn, so is the soul. By showing both forms of Nut, that which appears in the temple and that which appears in the grave, the card illustrates the way the Goddess acts for the individual person as well as the cosmos.

Like many other peoples the Egyptians established myths to "explain" the Sun's constant disappearance and return. These stories do not explain in the modern scientific sense, but rather express the way we experience and confront the mighty realities of nature. Different stories dealt with the Sun at night. As Ra, the Sun becomes old and simply dies. Myths that focus on Nut, however, tell us that the Mother eats the Sun in the evening, that it travels through her body and reemerges in the morning. In the Mother of Swords we see this event as the three red circles moving along the upright body. The number three reminds us of the Empress, just as the shape of arching Nut suggests the Ur Rune, and therefore the High Priestess.

Nut eating the Sun links her again to Kali, who on a much greater scale, "eats" the life energy of the universe, returning it to primal night. Unlike Kali, Nut is not the original mover of creation (at least not in the later myths that have come down to us). As we saw with the Ace of Swords, the first existence belongs to Nun, the dark chaotic waters. Atum (later joined to Ra) emerges, and the two together produce Shu and Tifnut, the wind and dew. And yet, other texts refer to Ra as the son of Nut.

The dew represented the primal pattern in the same way that Hagall, the hailstone, represented it for the much colder Scandinavians. When we learn that the Egyptians also compared Nut to a cow (linking her to Hathor), whose udder gives forth the Milky Way, we realize the remarkable links that exist between the African south of Egypt and the European north.

Pictures of Nut show her surrounded by stars, the way the Sky appears on a cloudless night. These stars always take the same shape, shown on the card. They resemble a human form with arms and legs out in celebration, the children of the Great Mother.

The pharaohs sometimes called themselves the sons and consorts of Nut. Pepi II described himself as living "between the thighs of Nut." Later images presented the pharaoh as sitting on the lap of Isis. The Egyptian word *nutrit*, for woman, meant "Little Goddess."

## DIVINATORY MEANINGS

In a reading Nut suggests someone mysterious, a private person who may seem distant or unapproachable to those around her. She can be very loving, even devoted, but she always keeps something of herself to herself. She maintains her own autonomy in all situations, even when passionate in love, or caring for her children. This may cause people to resent her, but if they do respect her need to keep something within, they will find that she gives greatly to those she loves. A person living out the myth of Nut will prefer night to day, the darkness to the light. She will care more for the sense of mystery than for explanation.

### REVERSED

Reversed, the Mother of Swords may show the need for privacy exaggerated. The person may find it hard to connect with other people, to respond to those who try to reach her emotionally. Alternatively it may show the person's need for autonomy threatened. She may find herself in a relationship with someone who demands too much from her. Or, she may feel a conflict in herself between her desire for quiet and mystery on the one side and her love for others, especially her children, on the other.

## FATHER OF SWORDS—RA

The figure of Ra thrusts us into the complex layers of Egyptian mythology. Like Brahma he probably began as the God of a particular class, the priests and pharaohs. In contrast with the popular Osiris, he seemed remote, somewhat like Brahma compared to Krishna. Later Ra became the supreme God—again like Brahma—and various other Gods, probably of different regions, became attached to him. We read of him as Amen-Ra, or Atum-Ra, or Ra-Harakhte, the figure we see on the card, with the falcon's head, which later became associated with Horus, the son of Isis and Osiris.

According to some creation myths, Ra created himself out of nothing. A certain hymn says he "came into being of himself." This same hymn, however, also describes him as the son of Nut. Thus

**Father of Swords in the South**
King of Swords

we find again the drama of the Emperor denying his origins in the Empress—that is, the patriarchal God claiming all power, including the essentially female act of creation, for himself.

According to some myths, Ra became old, for after all, he existed before all the other Gods as well as the world itself. Old, he became tired and so withdrew somewhat from his power and the world. As a result, humans rebelled. Ra gave his eye—which contained his power—to Hathor, who used the power to kill the sinful people. Finally, merciful Ra ordered an end to the slaughter. He established Ma'at, the concept of order and law, ruled over by Hathor. He then gave his power to Thoth to rule in his name and withdrew from direct involvement with the world.

Now, this story has many dimensions. Politically, it refers to the terrible chaos of the civil wars between the different kingdoms of ancient Egypt. Order and hierarchy became great virtues after such conflicts. From our modern standpoint, with our concern for liberation and democracy, Ma'at may seem to serve the ruling classes, the priests and pharaohs. Spiritually, Ma'at signifies right action in all situations. The reverence for order also reflects the tenuous existence of a people whose lives depended on the Nile periodically flooding its banks to irrigate the desert.

Ra's departure matches a mythological pattern found in many cultures. Students of religion call this pattern "deus absconditus," the God who withdraws. For many people creation occurs in stages. We find this in Greek myth (where the older generations of Gods were murdered by the younger), and in Scandinavian, and in lesser-known mythologies as far from Egypt as the South Pacific. In many places the God who creates the world gives the power to a younger group. We find a sense of this in Christianity, where God the Father becomes remote, giving His power, through the Holy Ghost, to the Son who enters the world of humans.

Ra represented the Sun. In the Father of Swords we see the great ball of the Sun (notice the spirally lines, like the trump) above his head. Some myths describe Ra as driving the Sun in his chariot across the ocean of heaven. Others describe Ra as the Sun itself. Each day Ra is born again out of Nut. As he travels across the sky he becomes old and finally dies, only to be reborn again the following morning. Some images of Ra show him in his night form, that is, dead, a mummy. We see him here as the powerful figure of the day.

In northern countries people think of the Sun in wholly positive terms. For Egypt, the Sun also brings death. The card depicts the Sun as huge and red. The deadly snake, the Uraeus or asp, curls around it. When Ra gives his "eye" to Hathor to kill the rebels, we can think of it as the desert sun. And yet, the Uraeus is green in contrast to the red disk. For even though the snake kills, it also symbolizes the mystery of rebirth. In the Haindl Tarot the green asp reminds us of the dragon in the final trump, the World.

As light and clarity, the Sun symbolizes order and law, but also life-giving energy, the *principle* of energy. Haindl compares Ra to the Native American idea of the Grandfather, the basic energy from which comes the Father, the more immediate God who acts in the world. Ra was the great-grandfather of Osiris, who fathered Horus. For the background of this vivid card Haindl has painted the colors of the light as he saw it in the Egyptian landscape.

Ra's symbol was the obelisk, which Europeans mistakenly think of as "Cleopatra's needle." Each day he sits there to receive the offerings and prayers of his people. But we have already learned that the Egyptians sometimes referred to the obelisk as Geb's penis. Clearly, the obelisk is a lingam, symbolizing male generative power.

Ra carries a scepter, symbol of his power (and also phallically shaped). The end is split, possibly for the union of the Upper and Lower Kingdoms. The split also means duality, with the joining symbolizing unity. We find the same idea in the Native American sundance, which requires a forked tree for the ceremony to begin. Ra also holds an ankh. As a kind of key, the ankh opened the mouth of a dead person to release the soul for its new life. The ankh has become a modern occult symbol, found in many Tarot decks, even those ignoring other Egyptian imagery.

On the right-hand side, vaguer than Ra himself, is the figure of a scarab, an Egyptian beetle. Scarabs characteristically roll balls of dung before them. In a marvelous act of the imagination the Egyptians saw this as a symbol of the world's creation. In yet another version of how the Sun makes its journey each day, some myths describe Khepre rolling the Sun before her as she travels through the sky.

## DIVINATORY MEANINGS

In readings the Father of Swords indicates a person who is dominant and autocratic. He tends to delegate authority to others, but ultimately they must answer to him. If the Emperor should appear as well, the two cards would bring out each other's arrogance. Other cards, however, might soften the Father of Swords.

The Father is a person of strong intellect, creative, yet in an analytical way, rather than intuitive. He insists on logic and can dismiss those who find logic difficult. But he will also listen to other people's arguments and be willing to change his mind. He values fairness as well as intellect.

## REVERSED

Reversed, the Father of Swords becomes jealous of his power. Like Ra, he will attempt to destroy rebellions by those he considers his "subjects." The powerful intellect turns to manipulation as he uses logic more to ridicule others and stay in control than to reach a fair analysis.

## DAUGHTER OF SWORDS—ISIS

With Isis we come to a figure of great importance in the occult tradition, and especially the Tarot. In many modern esoteric decks the figure of Isis (or her priestess) has replaced the female Pope as the second card. Her crown, the Sun disk in between the horns of a cow to symbolize the Moon, has become a standard image for polarity. We see it here not as an actual crown but as a double-image above her head.

The popularity of Isis goes back to Egypt itself, but continues through Greece into the period of early Christianity and as far north as the area around Cologne. She became the focus of mystery religions in Rome. The writer Apuleius quotes her as saying, "I am Nature, the parent of things . . . the first of the heavenly gods and goddesses, the queen of the dead." He then went on to give a list of the Goddess's names in different countries, ending with the statement, "The Egyptians . . . call me by my true name, Queen Isis."

To some extent the Greeks confused Isis with other Goddesses. They matched her with Aphrodite, the Goddess of love, whereas the true equivalent for Aphrodite/Venus was Hathor. At the same time, the Egyptians themselves tended to merge older deities into the current favorites, and some of Hathor's attributes became associated with Isis. The cow horns for the Moon come from Hathor. The Sun disk comes from Ra, for in the Osirian religion Isis forced Ra to give her his power, which she then gave to her son Horus. The eye of Horus replaced the eye of Ra. An Egyptian text reads "In the beginning there was Isis, oldest of the old."

The importance of Isis comes from two factors. The first is the Nile. Isis belongs astrologically to Sirius, which rises in the sky at the time of the annual flood. Isis, and Osiris, became associated with the life-giving waters, while Set, the evil brother, symbolized the desert, anti-life. In the Daughter of Swords we see her hair falling like water, with a suggestion of waves at the bottom. Like the hair of Gaia in the Star, Isis's hair contains the colors of the rainbow. The second factor was the association of Isis and her family with the afterlife.

Daughter of Swords in the South
Princess of Swords

Osiris became a kindly lord of rebirth, while Horus helped guide the souls on their journey. As mother and wife, as the heroine of the battle against Set (see the following card), Isis represented love, courage and devotion. Pictures often showed her feeding her infant Horus, a scene like the Christian Madonna and Child.

Isis became the mother of the pharaohs. Her name Eset (Isis is a Greek version) means "seat." To sit on the throne literally meant to sit on the lap of Isis. In the card we see an abstract picture of a throne above her head. Isis often appeared winged, with the wings often sheltering a small image of the pharaoh. The Egyptians saw the pharaoh as the authority, but the power of the land rested on the female. For this reason—and to copy the mythological patterns —the pharaoh married his sister. Above Isis's third eye we see the cobra, the regal serpent connecting the king to spiritual powers. The image suggests Shiva/Shakti and the kundalini snake.

The ribbon around Isis's hair shows a motif of doors. The cult of death often depicted painted doors. Since they were not real they could not open; only the dead spirits or the astral bodies of initiates could pass them. The occult tradition has developed the image of the veil of Isis, preventing the ignorant from seeing the secrets of the temple. The founder of theosophy, Madame Blavatsky, titled her work *Isis Unveiled*. In the Haindl Tarot, the image of the door joins Isis to the Empress as well as the High Priestess.

Unlike many other Egyptian deities, with their various animal heads, Isis was always shown as human (though at times with wings). This gives us a further clue to people's feeling of closeness to her. In the Daughter of Swords we see a naturalistic portrait of the Goddess as a young woman. The style resembles sculpture from the time of the Fifth Dynasty. To make their statues more realistic the sculptors inserted glass eyes. For the eyelashes and the eyebrows they used lapis lazuli, a stone that people believed came directly from the stars.

To the right we find Hathor, a shadowy figure in the background. An older figure, she somewhat merged with Isis in the New Kingdom. Hathor originally appeared as a cow, for people thought of heaven as a large cow, with the Milky Way pouring from her udders. (Thus we find the development Nut to Hathor to Isis—or did Hathor come first?) The cow body and horns vanished over time, but the ears remained the shape of a cow's. Hathor was the Goddess of love, dance and ecstasy. She also represented Ma'at, order—the opposite, in a way, of her other qualities. Because Hathor embodied female power, many of her statues later became disfigured, with the face often destroyed. Hermann Haindl has painted her whole, to symbolize the return of the Goddess. The colors of Isis and Hathor are red and blue—Fire and Water, mind and emotion.

## DIVINATORY MEANINGS

In readings, the Daughter of Swords indicates a powerful figure, confident and dynamic, who uses her power for some goal beyond herself. She is likely to be devoted to her family. Isis fulfills the traditional female roles of wife and mother. She is not, however, passive or dependent. Nor does she look to others for approval. She believes in herself and her purposes. Like the Empress, the Daughter of Swords combines sexuality with motherhood and devotion.

## REVERSED

Reversed, she suffers a loss of confidence. She becomes less sure of her goals or the rightness of what she does. The Daughter of Swords needs a purpose worthy of her strength and courage. Without this she can become depressed or confused.

## SON OF SWORDS—OSIRIS

Osiris was the first son of Geb and Nut. At his birth a voice proclaimed the "Universal Lord." Joy turned to wails of sorrow when the predictions came of Osiris's terrible fate. As ruler, Osiris taught agriculture to humanity. He was the enemy of violence and spread his rule throughout the world by gentleness and education. His brother Set, however (shown on many Wheel of Fortune cards as a snake curling downward on the wheel), became jealous and fashioned a conspiracy. At the celebration for Osiris's triumphs around the world, Set brought in a coffer and joked that it would go to whomever fit it perfectly. When Osiris lay down the conspirators nailed it shut and floated it down the Nile, heading out to sea. When we see Egyptian sarcophagi shaped to a pharaoh's body, we see a repetition of Osiris's coffin.

Isis recovered the body and brought it back. She copulated with her dead husband/brother (compare Kali and Shiva), and by her magic conceived Horus. Set acquired the body of Osiris and cut it into fourteen pieces (half the number of days in the lunar month). Isis searched the land and found thirteen of the pieces (there are thirteen months in the lunar year), all but the phallus, which a crab had swallowed. Carefully Isis reconstructed the body, fashioning a phallus out of clay, or wood. Then, with the help of Horus, Thoth and Anubis (the jackal-headed God also found on many Wheel of Fortune cards), Isis invented embalming, which gave Osiris eternal life. Having gone through death and come back, Osiris retired from the world to rule over the land of the dead.

**Son of Swords in the South**
Prince of Swords

Christians will no doubt recognize many elements of the story of Christ—the gentle teacher betrayed, resurrected and thereafter ruling over the souls who follow him through the passage of death. When we learn such details as the announcement by three wise men of his coming, or the fact that Egyptians ate cakes of wheat said to be Osiris's flesh, we realize that the ancient religion of Osiris inspired much of Christianity. According to historians, Osiris began as a God of vegetation, brought back to life by the Nile flooding the desert. Later, the people preferred to see him as the guarantor of their own everlasting life after death. One important difference from Christianity: Osiris belongs to nature as well as humanity. The three wise men are stars in the constellation of Orion. The belt of this constellation points to Sirius, associated with Osiris as well as Isis.

Just as most portraits of Christ show him crucified or arisen, so

Osiris usually appears swathed in white, the first mummy. Haindl's own picture comes from a grave painting in Deir el Medina, an artists' village. This card has become very personal for him, because at first he could not find an image of Osiris that truly inspired him. In a booklet he discovered a picture of the God in white, with a mutli-colored crown over a turquoise face, and an eye on either side. When he found the picture in Deir el Medina, it struck him that even if kings and the nobility were the only ones to have their graves painted, they still relied on artists to do it. And the work of the artist survives the work of the kings. The picture he'd seen in the booklet was painted in 1292 b.c., nearly thirty-one centuries ago. As an artist Haindl hopes that his Tarot deck will live after him.

His own version of the Deir el Medina Osiris appears surrounded by yellow light. The colors in the crown, blue and red, recall Isis and Hathor. Turquoise also suggests green, the color of new life, of Osiris as vegetation. Osiris carries the symbols of his rule, the flail and crook. Like Hathor, Osiris is a figure of order, authority, as well as eternal life. These symbols subtly connect him to the suit of Swords. The two symbols, with Osiris's head between them, form the Rune for Man, found on the card of the Devil. (Other pictures show Osiris with his arms crossed over his chest, another version of the same Rune, almost as if Osiris and the Runes indeed come from a single system.) Some commentators see this Rune as the power of human intelligence, the basic quality of Swords. Since the body of Nut (Osiris's mother) forms the Rune for the High Priestess, we can describe the High Priestess as the mother of the Devil. In the sense that the Devil symbolizes Shakti energy, and the High Priestess its source, the relationship gives us a new Tarot myth. We could, if we wished, create a story of the Goddess and her wayward son. As a figure of destruction, the Devil represents Set (both are shown as a snake). On a symbolic level, therefore, Set and Osiris, the great enemies/brothers, become two aspects of the same being.

## DIVINATORY MEANINGS

In readings, Osiris symbolizes someone gentle yet persuasive. He is highly intelligent and may be an initiate into esoteric mysteries, or at least someone with a strong interest in esoteric matters. Compared to Ra he does not demand agreement or argue aggressively, but instead convinces people, partly through his character. He is kind, and cares deeply for the people around him. At times, however, he may be weak, or naive, allowing others to take advantage of him. He may need the support of someone else—his Isis—to deal with anger or aggression.

## REVERSED

Reversed, the Son of Swords brings out the weakness, but also the possibility of corruption. He may turn into his evil shadow, his brother Set. This may come through having a position of power. The symbol of the flail, the whip, takes over from other apsects of the card.

# STONES—AMERICA

IN DESCRIBING THE blocs of power in the world, we use the term "West" to describe European and American culture and its off-shoots in Australia, New Zealand and elsewhere. This habit possibly originated in ancient Greece, where the idea of Europe itself first developed, as a cultural entity distinct from Asia Minor. When Europeans became more aware of India, China and Japan, they again divided humankind into Western and Eastern. But for Hermann Haindl, "West" means America, and America means the Native American traditions.

With the suit of Stones we come to the people who have so deeply influenced Hermann Haindl's spiritual development. Like many people Haindl thought of Spirit as something you heard about in church—an interesting, even important idea, but not a part of daily life. "Father, thou art in heaven" means, for many people, somewhere far away. From the Native Americans Haindl learned that the Great Spirit shows you how to live. Spirits are real, they live alongside us. In the sweat lodge he experienced their presence; he felt their touch on his body. Haindl does not think of himself as becoming Native American, nor does he wish to abandon his own culture. He believes instead that people can learn great lessons from Native America. We might call the main lesson "realism," for it teaches us to accept the sacred reality that lives in the Earth, that shows itself in the Sky and the Waters, that speaks to us in the Fires of life.

The terms "Native American" and "Indian" are both inadequate. First of all, both terms originate from Europe. They help maintain the distorted images Europeans have created over the five hundred years since Columbus. These images include "the noble primitive" and "the bloodthirsty savage." Like tribal peoples in other lands, the peoples of the Americas had a highly sophisticated culture, with developed ideas and philosophies. We can cite language as an example. In books and movies Native Americans usually say things like "Me give-um wampum," or "What say Great White Father?" It never occurs to white people that the Native Americans' command of English certainly surpassed white people's knowledge of Lakota, or Cherokee. Various people have pointed out that the philosophical subtleties of Hopi allow that language to express in words the transformations of quantum theory, something considered impossible by many physicists. Linguists have described the sign language of the Plains Indians—developed for communication between different cultures—as the world's only universal language, capable of communicating abstract discussions among people of different nations. As for "bloodthirsty"—some, not all, Native American cultures celebrated the warrior, but often as an expression of courage rather than violence. Among some tribes it counted more for the man to touch his enemy than to kill him. And some ethnographers maintain that most Native American nations valued peace much more than war.

The terms "Native American" and "Indian" also distort our impressions by painting the idea of one culture stretching across the Americas. Just as Europe consists of many peoples and languages, so America holds many nations, from the Iroquois to the Aztec to the Inuit to the Lakota. Just as the many European cultures tend to share certain characteristics, so do the Native Americans. We have already seen some of these, such as the reverence for the Earth, the recognition of Spirit in everyday life. But we should also respect the differences. As an example of sameness and variety, many Native Americans divide the world into four quarters based on the directions. For each direction they assign a color. However, the different cultures use different colors. The idea remains the same, but the details vary. The Haindl Court cards for the West show us different traditions, from the Hopi Spider Woman as the Mother, to Chief Seattle as the Son. They also show the connections between peoples; Seattle wears an eagle feather, linking him to the Lakota Daughter, with her feathered pipe. (We should mention here that the cards only show North America, for Haindl based them on his own experience, and he has not visited South America.)

The pictures on the cards do not come from actual paintings, like those of Wands or Swords. Instead, Hermann Haindl has created his own images, following the traditional symbols of the different nations. We see this most clearly in the Daughter, with her sacred pipe and three buffalos. Here, too, he has drawn on his own experience. Most people outside the Lakota nation know of this pipe from Black Elk's description of it. While in America Haindl smoked the pipe in a sacred ceremony with Black Elk's grandson.

White Americans tend to think of Native Americans as history. Those hostile to Native Americans speak heroically of "winning the West." Whites more sympathetic talk of the terrible tragedy that such noble people are disappearing. But the Native Americans have not disappeared. True, many tribes have vanished as separate groups. And a population of between twenty-five and forty million before the Conquest (these numbers come from Paula Gunn Allen's book *The Sacred Hoop*) has dwindled to something less than a million today. But the old ways have begun to come back, and with them the strength of the people. Many white people, when confronted with the crimes against Native Americans, tend to get annoyed. It all happened hundreds of years ago, they say. But the crimes continue today, with sterilization, forced resettlement, even murder of Native American activists.

If we think of Earth as the last suit, and the Son as the last card, then the deck "ends" with Chief Seattle. Thus it takes us from the spiritual abstraction of the Fool to a historical person. And yet, the two cards come together in a great circle. For in the Fool, Parsifal must learn to restore the wounded land. He must learn wisdom, symbolized by learning how to speak. As a man of wisdom, Seattle addressed the United States president. He *spoke* for the Earth and all her peoples.

## MOTHER OF STONES—SPIDER WOMAN

What a wonderful picture we see in the Mother of Stones. The serene face of the Mother radiating the labyrinth of her thoughts. The use of a labyrinth subtly connects the American Spider Woman to her Greek sister Ariadne, who gave her thread to Theseus so he could find his way back to the outside world after he had killed the Minotaur.

Many cultures have identified spiders with the Goddess. We see this in the common attribution of weaving to women, often as a sacred mystery. Just as the spider creates a web, an elegant pattern, so the Goddess creates the weblike intricacies and wondrous patterns of the physical world. Spiders and weaving also provided the models for the Scandinavian Norns and the Greek Fates, in both

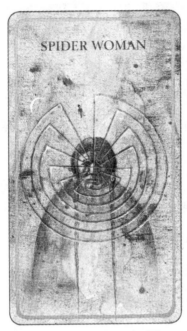

Mother of Stones in the West
Queen of Stones

cases three sisters who weave the thread of a person's life and then cut it at the right moment. The making of cloth from plants is a sacred act, for it transforms one thing into another. It brings greater organization and meaning into existence. It symbolizes the entire structure of human culture, which takes the materials of nature and creates things previously unknown. Because spiders spin webs out of their own bodies they form an image of the Goddess, who creates universes out of her own being.

Hermann Haindl has painted his impressions of Spider Woman from the Hopi accounts of creation. Spider Woman appears as a central figure in other American cultures as well, just as the idea of a "Great Spirit," or "Grandfather," shows up among different peoples. In the card of the Empress we mentioned the Keres deity, Thought Woman, whom Paula Gunn Allen links with Spider Woman. The picture on the Mother of Stones demonstrates the truth of that link, for the web radiates from the head rather than the womb.

Many Native Americans make a distinction between "Mother" and "Grandmother" as divine terms. Grandmother means the ultimate source, the potential for all things. Mother means the Spirit being who creates the world. In Tarot terms, we might describe the High Priestess as Grandmother and the Empress as Mother (though Thought Mother is Grandmother in Allen's account, with her twin daughters as the Mothers). The picture here reminds us of both cards. She stands very real and solid, like the Empress, while her long braids recall the gates of the High Priestess in traditional Tarot decks.

The inspiration for this picture comes partly from a Hopi prophecy about the fate of the Earth. Some of the ideas from this prophecy helped form such cards as Aeon. Hermann and Erica Haindl have the prophecy on a tape that also contains the Hopi story of creation. Like many other peoples, in America and elsewhere, the Hopis envision creation in several stages. They talk of humans passing through seven worlds, shown in the card as the seven layers of the labyrinth. Each of the earlier versions of creation broke down because the people could not sustain it. We now face the same kind of threat with this world.

The earlier worlds also broke down because of their own incompleteness. The world we live in now has emerged from the earlier ones. In some versions of the central myth, human beings begin in the center of the Earth and must follow a guide through various layers to the surface. This recalls the idea we saw in the Hermit and the Moon, that we live inside the Earth and have not yet reached the true outside.

The common belief around the world of creation in stages reflects an understanding that something so complex as the universe cannot have sprung into existence all at once. It needed to evolve through different levels. Many Native Americans see not only humans but other animals as vital for this evolution. In some stories a bird or a fish must bring up a ball of dirt from below the waters. This ball will become the Earth. We see many of the same themes we saw earlier in the Major Arcana—evolution as both a physical and spiritual process, evolution as incomplete, the responsibility of humans (and others) to carry it forward.

In the picture of Spider Woman we see a figure as archaic as

Gaia in the Star. She stands unmoving against a background in which the Earth and the Sky seem to join together. At the same time she is more accessible, closer to us than Gaia. We see her face. She looks like an ordinary woman. The use of a human term—grandmother—shows an intimacy with the Spirit world.

Hermann Haindl has said that he derived the pattern of the labyrinth from Hopi jewelry, which uses only silver, with abstract designs. This raises interesting issues, for the pattern exactly follows the famous Cretan labyrinth. If you trace it with your finger (beginning at the human entering the maze) you will find that it goes into the third level, then goes back out to the first ones, from where it works its way finally to the center. Once again, this suggests a spiraling evolution (and also the coils of a snake). We leap ahead, only to fall back and begin a slow progress to the truth.

Taken one way the little figure represents the creation, which begins with the Goddess, the center, and works its way through the stages to the outside. Taken another way it shows the soul entering the labyrinth, like the Fool entering the Major Arcana (to travel through 3 x 7 stages). Can we return to the sacred without losing our individual existence? Can we join with the Grandmother and remain ourselves? This question becomes more important as more and more people seek a new/old way of living in the world. There is no easy answer. We should recognize, however, that no monster lurks within this labyrinth, no ravenous beast from the unconscious waiting to destroy the conscious personality. Instead, we find only the calm face of the Creator.

## DIVINATORY MEANINGS

In readings the Mother of Stones signifies someone serene, probably older, with a great sense of her own being. She can be very loving, especially to her children, but she does not pressure them or demand that they demonstrate their love for her. She may at times appear remote, but this comes from her own self-confidence and the fact that she does not need approval from others. She does not rush about and may seem to move rather slowly. She cares more for nature than possessions.

Clearly, this describes an ideal. Not too many people will show all these qualities. The card may signify more of a principle than a particular person. It may show a person experiencing these qualities at a particular time or in relation to others.

## REVERSED

Reversed, the Mother of Stones shows a person who finds it difficult to be still and appreciate life. She may lack self-confidence or feel that she has lost her center. The reversed card carries a sense of being outside your own being, as if you stand beyond the labyrinth. Rather than run from one thing to another, or look for completion in relationships, she may find it necessary to slow down, to seek a way back through the layers of confusion. Reversed or right side up, the card carries a deep meaning usually seen only in the Major Arcana.

## FATHER OF STONES—OLD MAN

In the last card, the Mother of Stones, we mentioned the belief that various animals have assisted the process of creation. In some accounts, the Creator more or less says, "I've done my part. The rest is up to you." With such an attitude, humans do not see themselves as useless or insignificant. But nor do they see themselves as lords of creation, with all other creatures meant only to serve them. Hierarchy vanishes when we see the four-legged people and the people of the air and water working together with the two-leggeds to help create the world. In this picture we see not only the footprints of God, but also those of animals and birds and human beings.

Some people know the term "Bigfoot" as a legendary half-animal/half-man spotted in the mountains of North America, like the Abominable Snowman of the Himalayas. Here the name refers to the idea that we can never see God directly but only his footprints—the evidence of His presence in the world. The idea recalls the passage in the Bible where Moses can see God from the back but not the front. Another name for this Father is Old Man.

The same person who told Hermann Haindl he should use Brigid for Daughter of the North told him of Bigfoot. According to

**Father of Stones in the West**
King of Stones

his account, drawing a picture of the Old Man, or talking directly about him, is dangerous. Therefore, he said, people show his footprints. For Haindl, painting the Grandfather is not forbidden so much as impossible.

In the caves of Altamira in Spain we find pictures of hands and footprints. In the Father of Wands we also see a divine footprint. In India people often draw a design symbolizing the footprint of Shiva. Many people feel a need to leave their own prints in the cement of a sidewalk. In Hollywood famous stars leave their footprints outside a theater. All this shows the desire to make an impression on the world. In the Father of Stones we see various animals, but also the dark prints of a Spirit being. They, too, walk in the world beside us. For humans we see hands instead of feet. We affect the world more by what we do than where we go. Hermann Haindl has painted dark hands and light. He did this without any conscious purpose but we can describe it as symbolizing polarity. The prints appear in stone, not dirt. They will last. (In the Dome of the Rock mosque in Jerusalem, an indentation in the stone is said to be the footprint of Mohammed's horse as he leaps to Paradise.)

The Old Man is a helper Spirit for the Earth, taking care of the plants and animals. Hermann Haindl describes him as a Father, rather than a Grandfather. At the same time he also compares him to the Great Spirit (Wakan Tanka) of the Lakotas. According to Erica Haindl the Native Americans do not like to speak directly about Bigfoot, but will sometimes make jokes to outsiders. As with the intimacy of "Grandmother" these jokes do not imply irreverence. In the card we see yellow and orange light surrounding the footprints. The presence of the Old Man leaves the world filled with Spirit.

## Divinatory Meanings

When we discussed the Father of Stones I asked Haindl how he would interpret it in a reading. He described it to me as creative energy, and the fundamental male principle. As such, it becomes an archaic form of the Magician. Seen another way, the Magician takes the Old Man energy and focuses it. As a person the Father of Stones would signify someone who cares deeply for his family and those around him, as well as for nature. He is a hard worker, most likely a success. At the same time he can be difficult to approach or to know in an intimate way. He expresses his love more through action than direct warmth.

## Reversed

Reversed, the Father of Stones might exaggerate this last quality. People may find him cold and uncaring. Reversed also might indicate obstacles preventing him from achieving what he wants. He may suffer from a lack of success. Accomplishment matters greatly to such a person, though less for status than a desire to take care of his family. If he cannot do this—or if they reject his help—he may find his belief in himself shaken. Finally, the reversed Father of Stones might refer to someone pained at the suffering in the world around him. He may wish he could do more.

## DAUGHTER OF STONES— WHITE BUFFALO WOMAN

This card, one of the loveliest in the Haindl Tarot, expresses a central myth of the Lakotas. In his famous vision, Black Elk tells how two young men were out hunting when a beautiful woman approached them. One of them wanted to make love to her but the other recognized her as "wakan," holy. She was the Spirit of the Cow Buffalo (once again, the sacred cow, the animal found in all four directions). When the young men had escorted her to the community's sacred lodge, she told the people she had come to instruct them in the rituals. Above all, she had come to bring them the pipe.

The pipe embodies the cosmos: male and female (the bowl and the stem), stone and wood, the plants of the Earth and the Fire that transforms them. The red stem comes from the ground, while the buffalo head symbolizes all "four-legged people." The wooden stem represents all plants, while the eagle feathers represent the birds. The twelve feathers signify the months of the year. The person smoking the pipe becomes joined to the world (though we do not find Water). And when the smoke rises through the hole at the top of the lodge, the soul can follow the trail to the land of the Spirits.

When the woman had given the pipe to the tribal leaders she walked away from the lodge. After a moment she sat down, and when she rose she had become a red and brown buffalo calf. The calf walked a bit farther, lay down and rolled over, and when she got up she had become a white buffalo. A moment later, the white buffalo rolled over and became black. We see these three transformations in the card. The black buffalo bowed to the four directions, and then walked over the hill and out of sight.

As with the other cards in this suit we see the Daughter of Stones against a background of rock. A golden light surrounds her head, symbolizing the sacred energy. We see a young woman; she radiates a natural beauty. When Brave Buffalo told Hermann and Erica Haindl of the Sun Dance, he stressed that people of the Earth needed very little to fulfill their lives. Instead of vast funds for churches and giant bureaucracies, they needed only simple huts for the lodge, and a few small trees, plus stones and plants to make the sweat ceremony.

Hermann Haindl points out that there are two peoples called "Indian" in his deck. (Some time ago I read an article that claimed

**Daughter of Stones in the West**
Princess of Stones

Columbus was not thinking he had come to India when he called the people he met "Indians." The name "India" had not come into use in the fifteenth century. Columbus recognized that he had discovered a people unknown in Europe. He named them "in Dios," that is, with God, or living in a state of grace. I cannot judge the accuracy of this article but it does agree with the way Columbus described the Indians, or Native Americans, when he returned to Spain.) As East and West the two "Indian" peoples signify two poles. While India represents the elegance of culture, exemplified by Radha, America shows the simplicity of nature.

## DIVINATORY MEANINGS

In readings, the Daughter of Stones shows a person willing to take responsibility for something greater than herself. She seeks to help the people around her. She may show them how to help themselves. She demonstrates great love and courage as well as dedication. Her virtues include intelligence, for she understands the meaning of things and can explain them to others. A leader, she can inspire others to action. Her beauty comes from within. She is not a sophisticated person and may find herself uncomfortable in situations depending on elegance, wit or fashion. She cares more for nature than for art. As with the other cards, this picture is idealistic. The Daughter of Stones will more likely signify an aspect of someone, or a phase in a person's life.

### REVERSED

Reversed, the Daughter of Stones can indicate a person who seeks to inspire others but finds this difficult. She would like to help but does not know how to get across her ideas or emotions. The reversed card may show a simple person in an artificial environment. She may find herself out of place, with the wrong people.

## SON OF STONES—CHIEF SEATTLE

The Son of the West is the only Court card (and one of the very few in any deck) to show an actual person. He is Chief Seattle, one of the last leaders of the nation of people who lived along the northwest coast of North America. These people lived a peaceful life, based to a large extent on fishing, and hunting the orca, or "killer whale." We see in the Son of Stones a painting of an orca above the chief. The highly stylized quality of the painting shows that Seattle's people recognized the orca as a sacred beast, like the buffalo of the Plains Indians. Around the world tribal peoples have developed a spiritual relationship with the animals they hunted. As shown by cave paintings, this kind of relationship goes back tens of thousands of years.

When the white people came, anchoring their boats in the bay by what is now the city of Seattle, the Chief went to greet them. The whites were not unknown by then. Some who knew what the Europeans had done in other places told Seattle he would do better to make war, or run. But the bay was a sacred place, the site

Son of Stones in the West
Prince of Stones

of the yearly "potlach," when people would bring their valuable possessions to give to others (similar to the term "pot luck," the meal to which everybody brings a dish). And Seattle was a peaceful man. Possibly he did not wish to become a mirror of his enemies. He greeted the whites and invited them to share the land and the sacred fish God had given them. Today, only a scattered few remain of Chief Seattle's people. And the whales, all whales, are close to extinct.

The bay, and the area around it, remain closed. Despite the polluted air of the city, the power remains in the Earth.

Before his death, when it had become all too clear what the white people were doing to his people and to the land, Seattle made a speech to the United States president about the rights of the Native Americans. We have seen a fragment of this speech in the Four of Cups. He spoke not just of political rights, but of the Earth. The speech was a prayer; for traditional peoples politics and the sacred are inseparable. Today as well, Native Americans will pray before they make a speech. In the Indian movement to reclaim their land and their traditions, religion and political freedom once again have joined together. The original text of Seattle's speech no longer exists. We have only a later copy to tell us his message. Nevertheless, this message, at one time forgotten, has become more and more vital.

We see Seattle's face as if it has become part of the land itself. The face is rough, with the hair blending into the rock. Hermann Haindl has given him an eagle feather, a symbol from the Plains Indians. Seattle did not speak only for his own nation. A kind of lightning bolt comes down from the whale to the feather and the top of his head. The light indicates the bond between human and animal. A golden light shines around the orca, the same light that shone around White Buffalo Woman. It may seem strange to take for the Son a man who clearly acted as a father of his people. The idea of the Son is sacred. He brings the qualities of the suit into action. He is a Son of the Spirit.

The Court cards in the Haindl Tarot all complement each other. They show different approaches to the world. In discussing this card Haindl commented that Native America and Egypt are both old cultures, but very different. The Pharaoh carries a flail which can symbolize various things, but serves a literal purpose of whipping his people into obedience. Also, if we set the Son of the Earth alongside the Son of Fire, we find the image of a leader compared to someone who takes pleasure in the world and his own powers. The most striking contrast comes when we lay the Son of the West beside the Son of the North. Parsifal looks shocked at the discovery of what his people have done to the world. He faces the fearful challenge of his own responsibility to change. Seattle looks out at us with serenity and confidence. He understands his relation to the Earth, and he believes in his people.

Seattle and his people have suffered one of the most terrible fates imaginable: their land taken away (and abused), their culture ripped apart, their nation all but destroyed. And yet, Native America as a whole has not vanished. Not only have their traditional ways and knowledge begun to come back, they have seen their truths begin to transform the invaders who tried to swallow them. In the midst of their desperate situation many Native Americans remember that their people have lived in America for tens of thousands of years. Whatever has been done in the past four hundred, the land remains. And as long as the land lives, so do the people.

## DIVINATORY MEANINGS

In readings this most political of the Court cards becomes channeled into the idea of responsibility. The Son of Stones challenges us to work in society, to take action for the sake of positive change. According to Hermann Haindl the Native Americans say that a human being can do whatever he or she likes in the world—as long as he or she respects the needs of the next seven generations. The Son of Stones tells us to connect action to moral values. We must respect the Earth and the people around us. In the late 1980s, the prime minister of Norway headed a United Nations commission on the environment. When they made their report they insisted that environmental protection and economic development had to go together, especially in the poorer nations. Shortly after the report appeared, the prime minister spoke on the radio to people calling in with questions. Time after time, callers from all over the world tried to get her to say that the situation was hopeless, that nothing could move the powerful forces wrecking nature. Instead of despairing, she told them that action would make a difference. In her confidence and dedication she gives us a contemporary example of the Son of Stones.

## REVERSED

Reversed, the Son of Stones finds his confidence shaken. He listens to those who tell him to despair, or to those who say he should think only of himself. He may try to act selfishly. But he will not like it. At first, it may seem a relief to do only what he wants. At a certain point, however, he will feel lost. He will doubt himself or feel unconnected to other people and the world around him. Right side up or reversed, the Son of the Earth demands the same thing of us: action in line with reverence for the Earth and all Her children.

# COURT CARDS

|  | Image | Haindl Structure | European Structure |
|---|---|---|---|
| **WANDS** | Kali<br>Brahma<br>Radha<br>Krishna | Mother of Wands in the East<br>Father of Wands in the East<br>Daughter of Wands in the East<br>Son of Wands in the East | Queen of Wands<br>King of Wands<br>Princess of Wands<br>Prince of Wands |
| **CUPS** | Venus of<br>  Willendorf<br>Odin<br>Brigid of Ireland<br>Parsifal | Mother of Cups in the North<br><br>Father of Cups in the North<br>Daughter of Cups in the North<br>Son of Cups in the North | Queen of Cups<br><br>King of Cups<br>Princess of Cups<br>Prince of Cups |
| **SWORDS** | Nut<br>Ra<br>Isis<br><br>Osiris | Mother of Swords in the South<br>Father of Swords in the South<br>Daughter of Swords in the<br>  South<br>Son of Swords in the South | Queen of Swords<br>King of Swords<br>Princess of Swords<br><br>Prince of Swords |
| **STONES** | Spider Woman<br>Old Man<br>White Buffalo<br>  Woman<br>Chief Seattle | Mother of Stones in the West<br>Father of Stones in the West<br>Daughter of Stones in the West<br><br>Son of Stones in the West | Queen of Stones<br>King of Stones<br>Princess of Stones<br><br>Prince of Stones |

# READINGS

THINK OF THE Tarot as a very special kind of book, one which you can change every time you pick it up. By shuffling and laying out the cards you create a new order, and therefore new relationships between the cards. This widens the meanings of the individual cards, and therefore the whole deck. The Tarot is not just to study; we use the Tarot as a tool for self-knowledge, and for knowledge about the world.

People used to think of Tarot readings as a means of getting hard answers to direct questions: "Will I get the job?" "Will I get the girl?" Today we tend to see a reading more as a complex mirror of ourselves. A question about a relationship may show a person her inner attitudes to lovers and to sex. It may tell her something about how she behaved in past relationships, or how her upbringing has affected her, or what she really wants. At the same time, a reading is not entirely subjective. It does not show only the person's feelings and beliefs; it gives us a sense of what the patterns are in the world around us. What is the other person's attitude to the relationship? Does the moment favor the two of them getting together, or is this simply the wrong time? Among other things, the Tarot (and other oracles, especially the *I Ching*) teaches us to recognize that we exist in a complex pattern with the world around us.

Many people find it difficult to accept that the Tarot can give us any kind of objective view of ourselves, let alone situations. They wonder how a deck of cards can relate to outside reality. And if the person mixes the cards again, won't they say something entirely different? To take the last question first, in practice this tends not to happen. If you do the cards again, you usually get the same message, often with many of the same cards (people who have read through the card descriptions will realize that the meanings of many cards overlap, so that a second reading can give you a similar answer even with somewhat different cards). Very often there will be subtle but important differences between the two readings. In fact, the only reason to do it more than once is to gain greater clarity, or to see the situation from a different angle.

This still leaves the issue of why it should work at all. We should say first of all that the Tarot does not cause anything to happen. The cards do not contain some magic power to compel events. Instead, they reflect the direction events will probably take of their own accord. They show what a person is likely to do and what situations are likely to occur. More important, they give us a greater understanding of the situation right now, so that we can work to shape the future in valuable ways.

At any moment, the world and the people in it form a complex web. Think of the labyrinth radiating from the face of Spider Woman. There are forces we know of, and many more forces unknown to us. Together, the conditions and actions create reality. Now, a Tarot reading, or an *I Ching* hexagram, or a Rune casting, also creates a pattern. Because this small pattern exists within the larger one, it gives us a picture of the greater reality. It mirrors it. This may strike most people as a radical (and irrational) idea. We have grown up with the belief that events have to have a direct cause. If a tree falls over, something—a wind, or a bulldozer—must have pushed it. If two people in an office have a fight, they must have annoyed each other in some way. Now, the Tarot does not argue against cause and effect. It simply adds another dimension. It suggests that if the tree falls at the same time that the people are fighting, the two events go together. They help form a pattern, along with the other factors that make up that particular moment. By mixing the cards and laying them down, we allow ourselves to create a reflection of our own small part of the overall situation. The problem then becomes to interpret it.

The term "divination" literally means "to communicate with Spirits." We might term this the "archaic" view of readings. Because we do not consciously control the shuffle of the cards, we allow God, or Spirits, to guide our hands. Some people who cast Runes call on Odin to guide them. We do not need to believe in divine help in order to accept the value of a Tarot reading. We simply need to trust that the cards have a message for us, and then try to understand that message in the best way possible.

We should, however, recognize that the Tarot forms a spiritual philosophy. Anyone who has read the descriptions of these cards will understand that. This means that readings do not just advise us how to look for a job, or how to behave in a relationship. They also help us to see the world in a sacred way. Any method of creating a random pattern will give us some kind of reading. People have used tea leaves, dice, pebbles thrown on the ground, candle droppings, and so on. The value of the Tarot lies in the depth and subtlety of its messages. Because each card means something valuable in itself, the whole reading gives us greater understanding of the world and our own place in it.

Some people fear that if they believe in the Tarot, they cannot believe in free will. A Tarot reading does not eliminate choice. This is because it does not actually predict anything, not in an absolute way. It shows instead the likelihood of events. It says: given the current conditions, and the forces that shaped them, things are tending in certain directions. Actually, a Tarot reading can and should increase free will. Because it increases our knowledge, it enables us to make better choices. That understanding applies not just to ourselves, but to the moment. A reading may tell a person that conditions do not favor new relationships at this time; she will find greater fulfillment in a Hermit-like peacefulness. We see the idea, especially with the Minor cards, that a person needs to take action at some times, and to wait at other times. A reading shows us two things in particular: the first is our own motives and goals in a situation, and the second is the character of the situation itself.

There are many different ways of laying out the cards. Some people prefer to turn over a group of cards at random and see what they say. Most people, however, prefer to use a "spread," that is, a particular pattern. The cards go in a definite order and place, and the meaning of each card depends on the position as much as on the card itself. We will look at several of these spreads in a moment.

Whichever spread we use, the method of doing the reading remains roughly the same. The first thing is to decide on the question. You do not need to ask something very specific; you may wish to see what the cards have to tell you at this particular moment. However, if you do have a question, you should try to make it clear. This will help you to interpret the meanings. If you are reading for yourself, formulate the question in your mind or even write it down on a piece of paper. If you are reading for someone else, ask the person to tell you the question.

This last suggestion may surprise some people. They are used to the idea of the fortune-teller who guesses at a person's secrets.

It seems like cheating for the reader to know the question. However, we should not look at readings as a kind of game or test. We do them for understanding. If a reader starts off knowing the purpose of the reading, she or he can go much further in interpreting the answer. Still, there are some readers who prefer not to know the question. They wish to keep their minds as clear as possible for the moment when they first look at the cards. Others may wish to know the general area (love, money or spiritual development are the most common), but not any details. When you have gained some experience you will find what works best for you.

We should also point out that some people read only for themselves or only for others. It may sound easier to read for yourself but, in fact, many people find it much harder. First of all, you do not feel as involved when you read for someone else. If a disturbing card appears somewhere in the spread, you are less likely to panic. Or if something very nice appears, you can consider it more objectively when it concerns someone else. Also, when you read for another person you need to explain it. This means going slowly, discussing each card, and trying to find some overall interpretation. Through this process you carry your original impressions much further. You will see new meanings and new relationships between the different cards. When you read for yourself, you might stop at the first ideas that come into your mind. For a long time I never read for myself, but rather traded readings with a good friend. Only after some years did I learn to treat my own readings with the same care I give to others. Even now, I often prefer to ask someone else to read my cards. Doing so gives me an outside perspective on my questions and choices.

When the question has been formulated, the next step is choosing a "significator." This means a card to represent the person in the reading. Usually we choose this card ahead of time and set it on the table, face up, before the person mixes the cards. Traditionally, the significator is one of the Court cards. (Some people use a Major card, most often the Fool. For myself, I prefer to leave all the trumps in the deck.) In ordinary decks we might use a king for an older man, a queen for an older woman, a knight for a younger person of either sex, and a page for a child. In the Haindl Tarot, I would recommend using a Son or a Daughter. The simplest method is to find these cards in the deck and lay them out, face up. Ask the person to choose one, following his or her feelings about the picture. You can also choose the significator astrologically. As we saw in the Major Arcana, each sign belongs to one of the four elements. Therefore, a Leo would use the Daughter or Son of Fire. When the person has selected the significator, lay it on the table face up and return the others to the deck.

Now the time has come to mix the cards. The subject of the reading, sometimes called the "querent," shuffles the deck with the pictures face down. In this book I have given reversed meanings for each card. Therefore, the subject should shuffle the cards in such a way that some of them get turned around. One method involves setting the cards in a pile face down on the table, and then spreading them all around in a jumble, finally bringing them back together.

When the person has mixed the cards, he or she should lay them down again in a neat pile. With the left hand, the person cuts the deck to the left, then cuts the left-hand pile again to the left, making three piles altogether. The reader, also using the left hand, puts them back together with the bottom pile on the top. This separation into three is part of the tradition of readings. In the Haindl Tarot we can also think of it as a way of invoking the power of the Empress, who represents the Triple Goddess.

The reader then lays out the cards in the particular pattern called for by the spread. Some people prefer to turn them over one at a time, others to turn them over all at once in order to get a general impression before interpreting the individual cards. A little experience will show you the best method for yourself. When interpreting the cards, remember that the purpose is understanding, not demonstrating magical or psychic powers. If we trust that the cards have something worthwhile to tell us, then we need to give them the best chance to do so. This may involve discussing a card (or cards) with the querent. If you can see several possibilities, you might want to explore them with the person. Remember to use tact and caution if you think the cards say something difficult. Remember as well that a reading should be a positive experience. If the cards do show problems, try to find a way the person can use the experience. Do not lie or distort what you honestly think the cards are saying, but help the person deal with it in the best way. And remember that you are not infallible. Even if we accept that the cards will always reflect actual situations, this does not mean we will always understand their messages.

When you first begin to do readings, you may find it difficult to understand the cards at all. Many people find they can grasp what a specific card might mean but they cannot connect the different bits into an overall message. Do not get discouraged. Reading Tarot cards is a skill, and like any skill it takes practice. After you have done it for awhile, you will suddenly discover you can see things that would have completely eluded you when you first started.

At the beginning of your work with the cards, get yourself two notebooks. In one, record all the readings you do, with the date and a summary of your interpretation. If you remain in touch with the person, you can see if events match your impressions. And if someone comes back for a further reading, you can look at the previous one to see how the situation is developing. Very often in a series of readings, one or more cards will appear in each one. These cards will take on a special significance for that person.

In the other notebook, write down your own ideas about the cards. When you first get it, set aside several pages for each card. Write down your immediate impressions of the picture itself, and of the meanings given in this book. As ideas come to you about specific cards, add them to your notebook. A reading may suggest a new interpretation, or it may produce some strong feeling. If you meditate with the cards, you might record your experiences. In a separate section of the notebook, write down any thoughts you have about the cards in general. You might want to include pictures or stories suggested by the images. From time to time read over your notes. You will probably find yourself expanding old points that you wrote down months ago. Through this, and through practice with both readings and meditation, you will make the Tarot your own.

# SPREADS

There are a great many spreads for laying Tarot cards, and any book on Tarot will describe several. Some books devote themselves entirely to providing various spreads. Layouts include methods to link the Tarot to astrology, or to the calendar, or to Kabbalistic systems such as the Tree of Life, or to other esoteric diagrams. At one time, serious students of the Tarot dismissed readings as crude fortune-telling. Now that readings have developed into a serious tool for self-awareness, many excellent books exist which can help you put your knowledge of the Tarot into practice.

## THREE-CARD SPREADS

One of the simplest ways to begin Tarot readings is the use of three cards. The small number will help you see the connections between the cards. At the same time, a pattern of only three cards can sometimes produce remarkably subtle readings.

Here are two layouts, each using three cards. For both, lay the three cards in a row below the significator.

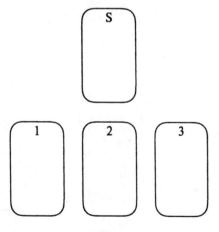

In the first method, card two, the center card, represents the current situation. It shows something happening in the person's life at this moment. Card one, on the left, indicates past experience, something that has led to the current situation. The third card, on the right, shows the future. This does not mean a fixed prediction, but simply the way things are heading. The person can change the direction (or help it along) through understanding the reasons why things are going the way they are going.

The other three-card method involves choices. Again the card in the middle depicts the current situation. This time, however, the cards on either side show two of the choices available to the person. An example will show how this can work in practice.

A person chooses Radha, the Daughter of Wands, as significator. Her question concerns a relationship, and when the reader turns over the cards they come out the Chariot, the Three of Cups reversed and the Daughter of Stones.

Daughter of Wands in the East
Princess of Wands

The Chariot

Overflowing
Three of Cups

Daughter of Stones in the West
Princess of Stones

Take a moment to look at the pictures. Allow the images to affect you. See if you can see their implications together. The following interpretation merely sketches the possibilities in this group of cards. The center card tells her that the situation has become overemotional. The intense feeling between the two people has spilled over into problems and sadness. The Chariot suggests that she can try to ride the wave of emotion, to use all that intensity to explore her own reactions to love and relationships. It implies a strong possibility of victory, that is, getting what she wants. However, she might find it a rough time, requiring courage and will-power. On the other side we find the Daughter of Stones. This would tell her to take a step back from the situation. White Buffalo Woman would suggest, first of all, serenity rather than high emotion. Secondly, it would advise her that she can find this serenity through putting her energy outside the relationship. Service to others may help ground her feelings.

The person in such a reading still might want to know the results of each of the choices. She can do this in two ways. She can do a more complicated reading (for instance, using the Celtic Cross spread described below), with a question such as, "What will happen if I follow the Chariot?" More simply, she can turn over two more cards, one directly under the Chariot, and the other under the Daughter of Stones. These two would then show the likely developments. Let us say the two cards are the Lovers upside down and the Hermit. The reading then would look like this:

Daughter of Wands in the East
Princess of Wands

The Chariot

Overflowing
Three of Cups

Daughter of Stones in the West
Princess of Stones

The Lovers

The Hermit

The Lovers reversed would indicate continuing problems in the relationship. The two people probably would stay together but without harmony. The struggles would continue for some time before they could become smooth again. The Hermit, on the other side, would carry the Daughter of Stones a step further. It would show the person feeling more peaceful, but it would also show her alone. She could feel good about herself and her world but without the other person. Notice that the cards do not offer any easy solutions. The choice remains difficult, but the reading might help to make it more conscious.

The above layouts are only two of the many possibilities for three cards. Another example might be one that shows the situation in the middle; on the left, the behavior of the person; and on the right, the behavior of other people.

## CELTIC CROSS

The most popular Tarot spread is probably the Celtic Cross, named for the shape formed by the first six cards. It appears in many books, usually with slight variations in each one. The version given here is one I have used for many years. After a person has mixed the cards in the usual way, turn over the first card and lay it on top of the significator. Lay the second card horizontally across the first.

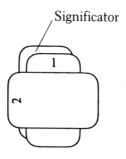

Significator

Turn over cards three through ten in the following pattern around the first two cards.

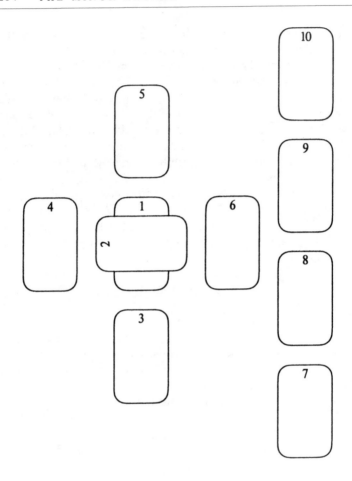

Cards one and two form the "small cross" or "center" cards. Cards three through six are the "cross," while cards seven through ten form the "staff." The meanings of the positions are as follows:

1. The Cover card—This shows the basic situation, the central issue.

2. The Crossing card—This card joins with the first card to state the concerns of the reading. Sometimes it acts as an opposition to card one. For instance, the Star, as a card of hope, might form an Opposition to one of the more negative Swords cards, such as the Five. The Crossing card also may show some result that has developed out of the first card. As an example of a result, suppose the

Cover card is Strength reversed, and the Crossing is the Five of Wands. This would indicate that the person feels weak at this time, and as a result gets into situations of conflict with the people around him. The Crossing card is always read right side up.

3. Basis—This card depicts some experience, usually in the past, that acts as a root, or cause of the current situation. Though it may indicate some specific event, it usually shows a more general condition that has led to the developments shown in the two center cards. Sometimes this card will reach deeply into the person's life. Once, in a reading about a woman's sexual difficulties, the Emperor in the Basis position brought up the issue of a stifling relationship with her father.

4. Recent Past—This card does not reach as far back as the Basis. It indicates what has been happening recently in terms of the person's question. It may show something that has finished but still affects the person. Or, it may show a continuing situation; in this case, the influence will probably come to an end fairly soon.

5. Possible Outcome—This card shows the *general* way things are heading. In contrast to the last card in the layout, the Outcome (see below), it is less specific and less definite. For instance, an Outcome of the Son of Cups might indicate a decision taken about something, while the Possible Outcome of the Universe suggests that the decision is apt to turn out quite well.

6. Near Future—This card indicates immediate developments. It is not the final result of the situation, but part of its unfolding. Like the recent past, it tends to show conditions that will not last. If the card indicates a problem, the reader can point out that the difficulty will be temporary. If it shows something desirable, the reader can advise the person to make the most of it while it lasts.

7. Self—This card shows what the person contributes to the situation. It may show an attitude or an action. You may find this the key card, as in a reading I once did where the Chariot reversed showed that the person lacked the will to continue in the situation.

8. Environment—This card shows influences from outside the querent. It may refer to some specific person (especially if the reading concerns a relationship), or to the general atmosphere.

9. Hopes and Fears—This card illuminates what the person expects to happen. Often this position greatly affects the Outcome because it shows the person's attitudes and desires. For instance, the Five of Swords here would say that the person fears defeat; such

pessimism can help bring about that defeat. The Star would produce a much more positive result. This position sometimes helps the person confront hidden attitudes.

10. Outcome—This card sums up the other nine. It shows the most likely result, given all the other influences.

We should never consider the result as fixed. We can always change direction, and in fact, the reading itself, because it shows the way things are going, can serve as the starting point for change. The very fact of having a reading means that the situation is no longer the same. Still, we should not assume we can alter that situation without any serious effort. A reading may show strong influences on a person's life. Going against those influences can demand conscious work. If the reading should show some sort of undesirable outcome, the reader should help the person find ways to improve the situation.

## THE WORK CYCLE

Tarot spreads give you information. At the same time they give you images of your life. You can use these images to focus your efforts at change. However, most readings primarily tell you what is happening. The spread below, developed by myself, emphasizes what you can do in the situation. Unlike most layouts, it also provides a method for turning over more cards if the first line leaves you without a clear answer.

Choose the significator and mix the cards as usual. Lay the first card on top of the significator and the second across it, as in the Celtic Cross. Then turn over the next seven cards in a row below the first two.

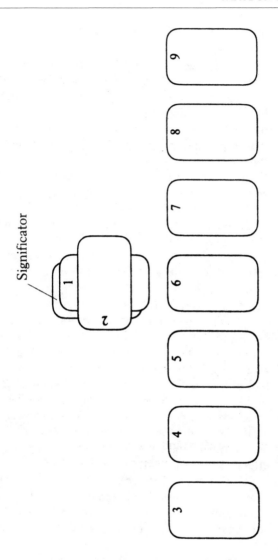

Cards one and two set out the same basic situation as the first two cards in the Celtic Cross. Card three refers to Past Experience. It shows part of the background to the situation. It acts somewhat like the Basis in the Celtic Cross. Card four represents Expectations. It indicates the person's attitude, what he or she expects to happen. This helps to identify positive or negative approaches. These are not always conscious. The next three cards, five, six and seven, are read together as the Work. They indicate the opportunities and obstacles facing the person.

The sixth card is the Outcome. It shows what is likely to happen. The seventh card is the Result. It indicates what will happen *because* of the Outcome. For instance, suppose that card six, the Outcome, is the Two of Swords. This indicates a truce between people who may have been having problems. But what will happen after the truce period ends? Will they stay close or go back to quarreling? The Two of Stones as the Result would indicate that the truce allows harmony to develop.

If these cards give you a clear message, then stop there. But if you find yourself still seeking understanding, you can lay out a second line of seven cards underneath cards three through nine. The same positions apply to this second line of cards. As a group, they will show a different aspect of the situation, giving the person a chance to look at it from a different point of view. Often the point of view is defined by the first two cards in the line, the Past Experience and the Expectation. For instance, if these show a realistic attitude then the Work and the Results are likely to be positive. But if the Expectation card indicates over-optimism, or exaggerated fears, then the rest of the line may become distorted as well. The Work may call for the person to see the situation as it really is.

In principle you can lay out up to ten lines, with five cards left over for a "commentary." In practice, I have rarely found the need to go beyond two or three lines. For many readings, the first nine cards will give a firm answer.

This spread works best with questions such as, "What should I do about my problem?" or "What is the best way to handle . . . (a person, an opportunity, etc.)?" You might ask, "What approach can I take to get the job?" or "How can I deal with my lover?"

## THE HAGALL SPREAD

A new Tarot should have a new spread. In working with the Haindl Tarot it struck me that one thing that distinguished it was the way the three types of cards had their own character. A layout especially for this Tarot could reflect this, with the Major Arcana and the Minor Arcana Suit cards and Court cards, each shuffled and laid out separately. When I created this layout, and was working out ideas for the Minor Suit cards and the Major cards, I discovered that together they could form the Rune Hagall—so important as a symbol for the entire deck.

To lay out the Hagall spread, first separate the cards into Major, Suit and Court cards. You will then have three piles. The spread does not call for a significator, so you should not remove any cards.

Begin with the Suit cards. Shuffle the forty cards, as usual thinking of your question. When you have mixed them, turn over four cards in a diamond pattern.

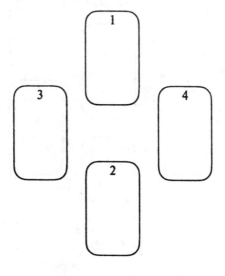

Suit Cards

These cards describe what is happening. Card one indicates the general situation. Card two, below it, shows something you've done, or an experience you've had, that has helped create the current conditions. Card three shows your beliefs—your own impressions and expectations, conscious or subconscious, of the situation and where it's going. Very often, our beliefs shape the situation in a much greater way than we realize. This card can help you see those beliefs and decide if they work for you or against you. You can follow through on them or change them. Card four indicates the likely results of the situation as it stands now.

We next go on to the Major cards. Mix up the twenty-two trumps and lay down three in a triangle above the Minor cards. This creates Hagall.

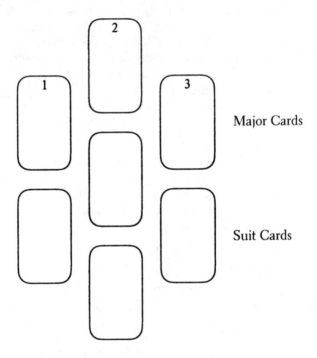

Major Cards

Suit Cards

The Major Arcana indicate our spiritual tasks in life. Some of them challenge us, like the Chariot, the Hanged Man or the Devil. We may have to overcome obstacles, either in ourselves or in the outside world, in order to fulfill these challenges. Other cards, such as the Lovers, or the Star, come to us as wondrous gifts. The task with these cards becomes to appreciate them, and to use them in a way that helps us but also helps the world. In the triangle, card two, on top, signifies the spiritual task at this time. It shows the challenges and opportunities in the current situation as shown in the Suit cards. Card one, on the left, represents spiritual history. It indicates something about how you've behaved in the past, and what you've learned. Card three, on the right, indicates a "metamorphosis." It shows, on a spiritual level, how the situation will change, and the spiritual tasks that will come to you as a result. You might look at it as connected to card four of the Suit cards section, the likely results.

Now we come to the Court cards, possibly the most interesting aspect of this spread. Mix them up and set out three cards in a row below the others. The final pattern will look like this:

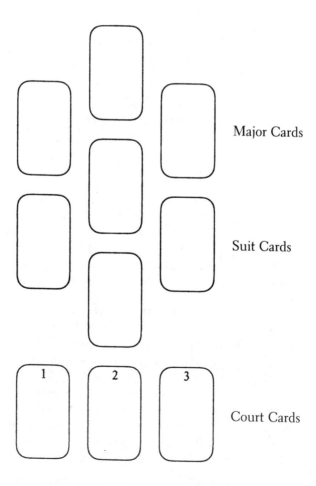

In this reading, the *Court* cards are always read right side up. If they come out reversed, turn them around before interpreting them. The card in the middle shows you yourself. It indicates what aspect you have taken on in this situation. It does not say you have actually become Radha, or Osiris, but only that you are expressing those qualities at this time. We can describe the Court cards as various ways of being in the world. At different times, and in different situations with different people, we will probably experience all of them. The card in the middle shows you which one you are experiencing now.

Card three, on the right, symbolizes the Teacher. Here we do think of the card as the person. If Brigid comes up here, look at her special qualities and imagine her as an actual Teacher. Imagine the demands she would make on you and the help or instruction she would give you in this situation. Brigid would make a fairly gentle Teacher. Odin, on the other hand, or Kali, would be very demanding, possibly fearsome. And yet, think of all you could learn from a figure like Odin.

Card one, on the left, symbolizes the Helper. Again, visualize the actual person shown on the card. Only now, instead of someone who instructs you or challenges you, this person gives you total support. She or he will help you to deal with the conditions shown in the Suit cards, and the spiritual tasks shown in the Major. Think of the myths and fairy tales in which Athena, or Ariadne, or Merlin, or simply a kind animal in the woods, helps the hero accomplish some impossible errand. As a Teacher, Odin would push us very hard. Because Odin is a trickster, he might put us in situations where we could not know for sure what is happening. As a Helper, however, Odin would lend us his great power. We could allow ourselves to feel magical in the situation, with access to wisdom. By contrast, with Radha as your Helper you could allow yourself to look at everything more lightly. You could feel relaxed and sensual.

Clearly, some Helpers are stronger than others. Parsifal would give you less magic than Kali. But maybe you do not need Kali at this time. Maybe Parsifal, with all his own doubts, is just right for you. To feel that your Helper remains with you, you might carry the card in your pocket, or bag. Or you might draw your own version of it and carry that with you. If you prefer words to pictures, try writing (or telling yourself) a story with the Helper (and perhaps the Teacher) and yourself as characters. This last exercise can be valuable in helping you see fresh possibilities in the situation.

This reading treats the Court cards in a very different way than most spreads. It takes them beyond the strictly psychological and looks at the Gods and Goddesses as living beings. Some people will prefer to see this as aspects of themselves (or people around them). Others may go wholly in the other direction and see them as genuine divinities. Still others might take a middle approach, looking at Spider Woman, or Osiris, or the Goddess of Willendorf, as patterns of energy which we personify in human terms. Remember, too, that one of the three cards indicates yourself. This can help you strike a balance between the personal and the mythological aspects of the images. Whatever your approach, try the Hagall reading and see how it affects you.

# MEDITATION

**M**EDITATION WITH THE Tarot allows us to create a personal bond between ourselves and the cards. Sometimes meditation will come out of a reading. The person lays out the cards and one card strikes her or him as very important. Usually, this will be one of the Major cards, or a Court card, for these pictures present us with powerful mythic images. We see the Magician in our reading, we recognize its importance at this time in our lives, and now we want to go beyond simply understanding what it means; we want to gain a genuine experience of the Magician's creative power. And so we do a meditation with the Magician, and in this way enter into the world of the image.

Meditation does not have to depend on readings. You can choose a card that seems valuable to you at a particular time. Also, many people who study the Major Arcana follow a program of meditating with each card. If they follow a Kabbalist teaching, they will likely connect these meditations to the twenty-two pathways on the Tree of Life. But we do not need to use such a strict program in order to work with the trumps. We can enter into the images of cards one by one, or in groups. One worthwhile meditation with the Haindl Tarot uses the Chariot, the Hanged Man, and the Star as a trio.

Meditation gives us a non-rational experience of the cards. It takes us directly to the heart of the image, allowing us to make it a part of our own lives, our own knowledge. Each card has its own qualities, so that joining with the Moon, for instance, is a different experience than joining with the Magician. Two people doing the same meditation with the same card will not receive the same images and feelings; they will, however, share in the particular values of that card.

Probably, you will not achieve this "joining" right away. You might find in your first tries at meditation that you keep getting distracted, or your mind wanders off in completely irrelevant directions, and nothing at all seems to happen between you and the picture. Unless you actively dislike it, keep trying. Slowly you will discover that your relaxation is deeper, your contact with the cards more intense, and your experiences more personal. Meditation brings many other benefits besides a greater understanding of the Tarot. It gives you a more centered approach to life, a more relaxed attitude to problems, and an opening to the sacred dimensions in your daily life and the world around you. Meditation can widen your perceptions while at the same time grounding you in the immediate reality of your own breath.

There are various kinds of meditation with Tarot cards. However, they all begin with a deep relaxation. This allows you to clear your mind of all the usual thoughts, worries, tensions, excitement, and so on that tend to fill our days. Relaxation brings its own rewards. It calms the nerves, it renews the body and opens up the breath. But it also makes room for the spiritual messages contained within the cards.

To begin your meditation choose a time and place where you can sit comfortably without disturbance by family or visitors or outside noise. For some people, such as parents with little children, this may require a special effort. However, meditation need not take longer than fifteen minutes to half an hour. If you decide to do a regular program of meditation try to do each one at the same time and in the same place. Sit in a comfortable position with your back straight. Try to sit in such a way that you do not draw your knees up to the chest, for this restricts the breathing. You can sit in a straight chair, or cross-legged on the floor. Make sure to find a place and position where you will not feel the need to move constantly, for this will distract you from the meditation. If back pain or some other problem makes it difficult for you to sit comfortably, lie down, preferably on the floor and without a pillow. You want to keep the spine straight.

If you think you might want to end the meditation by writing in a journal, or by drawing something, have whatever you need alongside you. This prevents breaking the meditation by having to get up and search for paper or colored pencils. Some people have a special object that contains for them a sacred power. This could be a ritual object, like a wand or a pentagram, or else a crystal, or a stone. If you have such an object, you might wish to include it in your meditation, placing it alongside the card, or holding it in your hand.

Begin the meditation by letting yourself sit peacefully and calmly. Close your eyes and feel that you are coming to a rest. Let your breathing lengthen out, let it become deeper and easier. Do not force it, but allow the breath to go all the way down to the diaphragm, and when you let it out, release all the breath from your body before you take another one. Continue to focus on your breathing, and with each in-breath allow calm and peace to fill your body. With each out-breath, let all distractions and worries float away from you. Feel yourself begin to relax. Let go of the tension most of us carry in our bodies, especially in places like the shoulders, the neck, the back, the bridge of the nose, the jaw. Let your breathing carry it away from you.

Probably the simplest meditation with the Tarot involves taking the qualities of the card into yourself. This meditation works well with cards that have come up in readings, or cards you feel you need at this time. If your life seems scattered and you find yourself weak, you might choose to meditate with the card of Strength, or the Hanged Man.

When you are sitting comfortably and ready to begin, take the card into your hand. Look at the picture. Do not seek to analyze it or memorize any of its official meanings. Allow yourself to experience its qualities. You might want to think of a time when your life did express this kind of energy, or peacefulness, or wisdom. Imagine what you could do in your life now if these qualities came back to you. Now put the card down again, sit relaxed and close your eyes. As you begin your relaxation do not try to remember everything you were thinking. Release it along with all the other thoughts crowding your mind.

When you feel yourself relaxed, allow the image of the card to come back into your mind. Do not worry about the accuracy of your mental picture. Now as you breathe in, let the qualities of the card fill you with each breath. And as you breathe out, experience those qualities moving through your whole body. Some people like to imagine pure light surrounding them and the card. This helps to deepen the bond between themselves and the image. When you feel you have spent enough time with the card, take a final deep breath, and when you release it open your eyes.

Sit for a while longer before you go back to your regular activities. Pick up the card again and look at the picture. You might want to repeat the meditation several times over a period of days. Eventually you will find that in the middle of other activities you only need to think of this card in order to draw on its special qualities.

A more complex form of Tarot meditation involves a kind of story created with the cards. In the description for the Star, I referred to a meditation I led in Haindl's studio in Hofheim. In this visualization, which was based on the Hanged Man, the people saw themselves climbing a tree that became larger and larger the higher they climbed, until it opened up into the World Tree itself. When they reached a certain point they imagined themselves tying one foot to the tree branch so they could hang down, with the sky and the branches of the tree behind them. Far below they saw the old woman washing her hair, and as the clear water ran over the rocks they allowed themselves to experience the hope of renewal in their own lives.

Meditations such as this usually require a teacher, not for expert knowledge, but simply because people need someone to act as guide. The meditation works best when you sit or lie without moving or thinking, and open your imagination and feelings to the images given to you by the guide. You want to see the Tree; you want to see yourself in the branches, and the light of the stars shining on your hands. If you have to stop and think of what should come next, you lose that quality of staying completely within the experience. If you wish to do such meditations by yourself, you might find it best to tape the instructions beforehand. Think of the kind of story (myth) you want to create. Do not make up too many details ahead of time or you will leave no room for spontaneous experience. However, you should include directions like, "Feel the bark of the tree under your hands. Smell the air, and hear the sound of the birds." Just as in a written story, these sensual details give the experience a deeper reality. Only here, you will create these details yourself.

When you have worked out the various steps, record them on a tape, speaking softly but in your natural voice. In between the different stages of the story leave time for the spontaneous details to come into your mind. Then, when you wish to do the meditation, simply do a relaxation (the same as described above) and play the tape.

All this will take some experimenting. You will need to find out how fast to speak, how much time to leave, how much description to include, and so on. However, it should not take too long to find the method that works best for you. Various books give transcripts of these kind of meditations. (Other terms you might see are "guided fantasies," "visualizations," or "pathworkings.") You can read them into a tape recorder and then play them back in the usual way. You also might want to form a group with other people studying the Tarot. As well as discussing what you've learned, and reading each other's cards, you can take turns leading meditations. Besides the benefits of the meditations themselves, this will give each person the experience of being a teacher as well as a student.

A meditation that has become a tradition with the Tarot calls for you to enter the card itself. For some people this can mean actually projecting yourself out of your body. Such a drastic exercise is not necessary, however, to gain a valuable experience with the images. Begin your meditation in the usual way, looking at the picture and then setting it down to do a relaxation. When you feel yourself ready, pick up the card again. With the eyes still closed, feel it in your hands. Try to see the image in your mind, creating as much detail as you can. Staying in the meditation, open your eyes and look at the card. Notice any ways in which your image didn't match the actual picture. Now close your eyes again, and once more construct the picture in your mind. When it seems complete to you, let the picture get larger. Imagine it expanding in front of you until it becomes larger than the room. Let it become life-size, not as a two-dimensional card, but as an actual scene, with real people and objects. Without actually moving, imagine yourself getting up and entering the world of the picture.

Take a moment to orient yourself. As with the story meditation above, let your senses awaken to this new place. Feel the ground under you, smell the air, hear whatever sounds there are. Allow the scene to change. Maybe the people are doing something, or talking to you. Maybe someone new will enter the scene. Do not choose consciously what is going to happen; instead let yourself experience whatever comes. If you find yourself taking part allow this also to happen spontaneously. When you sense that the scene and the actions have done what they needed to do, take a step back. Return through the "door" of the picture back to your place in the room. Now see the scene shrink back to the size of a card. When it has done so, let the picture dissolve. Then, when you find yourself ready, take a final breath, and when you release it, open your eyes.

You can use this meditation to create your own Tarot card. Before you begin the meditation, take a large sheet of paper and several colored pencils or felt-tip pens, and set them beside you. When you have returned from the world of the card draw, or write, what you experienced there. Your picture may end up very close to the original version, or something entirely different. You can, if you like, do this for the entire deck, or the trumps, or simply for those few cards which have become most important to you. However you approach this or other meditations, they will give you an understanding of the cards unlike any other.

# EPILOGUE

## The Haindl Tarot Is the Mirror of a Life-Story

THERE WERE SIGNIFICANT points in his life when Hermann Haindl began the paintings for his Tarot cards. These cards are central to his artistic work and it is useful to take a look at the roots of their development. The Haindl Tarot represents a summary of Hermann Haindl's life. It can be compared to a tree, which lives with its roots and branches through the uncountable places of contact with the material and non-material world.

It was in 1945 that Hermann Haindl, a 17-year-old, fell into the troubled confusion of the last months of World War II. Still a youth, he became a soldier for a brief time. He was captured and then held as a prisoner of war in Russia for four years. He belonged to a generation of young people torn away from home and seemingly discarded. Seldom has a generation of young people been sacrificed in a more criminal manner.

It is difficult to find any philosophically creative meaning in imprisonment: 170 young men had gone off as one company; only three survived. Hermann Haindl was one of the survivors. In the unfolding of his life story, this period of constant closeness to death was of utmost importance. During this critical adolescent phase of forming an identity, Hermann Haindl found himself catapulted to the very edge of physical and psychological existence. During this time he experienced a profound religious conviction of the awareness of the life force within us, the energy we call God. It gave him the strength to live through all the obstacles and horrors he faced. To this day, he has lived his life out of this perpetually full well. While his way of life is often unsettling to others, it is both humble and upright.

If suffering can have a creative meaning, Hermann Haindl's life and work were formed by it. While there is no justification for the insanity through which he acquired his experiences, it gave him a passion for working toward peace and reconciliation with the environment of our planet.

Throughout our life together, Hermann has spent long hours telling me about the years of imprisonment. In those times, experiences with death were an everyday occurrence. Once, he had to dig his own grave. Many times, his life was saved by strangers. Between the hope for mere survival and the recognition of a higher life principle lay many small encounters with nature, with other people and with himself. These shaped his life and made inner growth possible. Within him grew an autonomous law of life that gave him independence from the opinions of others.

A central theme in the ever-returning memories of prison is a little birch tree. The barren land of the huge camp was surrounded by high barbed-wire fences and guard towers. Successful escape was unthinkable. Others had fled, only to be brought back and shot before the eyes of their fellow prisoners. The future was uncertain and covered with darkness, but those who gave up died.

One day, as Hermann often tells, he discovered a tiny birch shoot just outside the fence. Day by day its new leaves unfolded and stretched further into the light. Throughout a spring and summer the birch shoot grew into a small tree. For hours at a time Hermann sat and contemplated the young tree. The sun and the rain fell equally on the little birch and on the barbed wire. The tree—growing in the midst of misery and the destruction of human dignity—became a symbol of rebirth and life for Hermann.

The message of the simple birch shoot to the young man behind the barbed wire was fundamental: "Live. Believe out of your center, like I do, in a cosmic energy that gives us strength and abundance."

As a refugee in 1949, the way back into the emerging and already prospering society of post-war Germany was long and difficult. Hermann Haindl never forgot the green leaves of the little tree, even though this memory was often veiled by the ordinary difficulties and worries that can go with making a fresh start. But once acquired, the secret of the profound connection between life and death became a well of strength in him, never to be lost.

At the end of the sixties, Hermann reached an artistic crisis. Since the war, a focus on progress had brought prosperity for many; the years 1968–69 brought up for the first time deeply repressed fears and despair, and—resulting from them—some new hope. Hermann Haindl had been working for a number of years as a stage designer and head of the artistic workshop in the theater in Frankfurt. The intensity of that creative experience became a model for him for action within society. In the face of emerging social turbulence, painting abstract pictures lost its meaning for him. For a whole year he touched neither canvas nor brush.

When he returned to creative work he was a different person. The life and suffering in Russia under extreme circumstances shone through all his work and became a dominating principle. In 1970 the painting "The Eye" was born. This work signifies the beginning of the new creative period that culminated eighteen years later in the Haindl Tarot cards.

By 1985 Hermann and I had lived together in Hofheim for thirty years. In an address at an exhibition celebrating our anniversary, Ingrid Mössinger said: "The first painting after this inner emigration was appropriately named *Eye*, as the window of a new consciousness. Whereas Hermann Haindl's view of the environment was originally fastened on the surface of things, losing itself in increasingly abstract forms, in 1970 he turned his focus intensely to the reality of the environment and of nature. The difference between his earlier and later work is a difference in depth: the focus is not on capturing the part of nature comprehensible to the 'eye,' but on the character of the natural. Rather than an interest in what the individual, physical eye perceives, it is the archetypical in nature that has gained importance. In a manner of speaking Hermann Haindl looks with archaic eyes into the soul of nature. . . . Hermann Haindl turns . . . with the voice of his paintings against prejudice and restrictive thinking. He pleads for unhindered and exuberant growth in nature" (Ingrid Mössinger: Hermann Haindl, 30 Jahre in Hofheim, Catalogue for the exhibition, 1985).

One section of this painting, which stands at the wake of the new beginning, has become the leading motive for the seventy-eight cards of the Haindl Tarot. The eye looks at us from the back of the card. It is not the timeless, seeing eye of a godlike entity—this eye is marked by suffering. Amid the otherwise immaculate beauty and tranquility, an abscess must be endured. The abscessed eye presents a symbol.

Perhaps only through suffering can we reach a higher state of awareness, one in which the language and the message of a birch tree becomes comprehensible.

The Haindl Tarot is also the origin of a further step in the life of Hermann Haindl. In 1980, after exactly thirty years to the day, Hermann Haindl left the theater entirely to begin working on his own. It was a Friday afternoon, and on that same day I received word that I had lost a job that had been promised to me, which was to have supported us for several years. It was quite a shock. Hermann sat with me and comforted me. Two hours later he got a phone call in which he was told that a big commission we had counted on had been given to somebody else. It was a true "Tower" situation. I will never forget that afternoon. But after that sudden collapse of our material security, Hermann said, "This is supposed to happen. Now I will finally have time to paint my own Tarot cards!"

So began one of the most suspenseful phases of our joint lives. In unimaginable intensity, one Major Arcana card after another emerged. Each one was more beautiful and exciting than the last.

Long, intense conversations filled the days and weeks as, with merciless intensity, Hermann pulled all the people close to him into the suction of his constantly growing creation.

The first card to come about was the Wheel of Fortune. Truly, it had whirled us off the ground. This card, very reserved in the colors, shows Hermann Haindl's life principle symbolically. The axis of the wheel is the very center of the personal life. However, to know one's own personal center is to confront pain. Hermann's Wheel of Fortune depicts this theoretical and philosophical concept of life; but in particular it shows a life that has been deeply experienced and suffered through, as some of the consequences of war and imprisonment are ongoing pains and limitations that Hermann Haindl endures.

So far, it has been a basic experience in our life together that whatever we need comes in abundance. Now, not only the paintings that were completed since 1970, but also those from our travels over the past years—to Ireland, Scotland and England, to India, and including the many contacts with the Native American people of North America—turn out to have been part of our journey to the Tarot deck. The puzzle has now come together. In fact, the pieces had always belonged together, but these connections were hidden from us.

A last and very conscious piece completed the picture—a trip to Egypt in early 1988. Our immersion in that culture and the way it touched us were profound and overwhelming. Here were Nut and Ra, Osiris and Isis—out of the exalted sublimity of a 5,000-year-old history emerged faces distinguished by the timeless beauty of the Gods. We saw these faces vividly in the throngs of people everywhere in present-day Egypt. They surrounded us in cities and villages, passed us by, treated us with empathy, and sensed their way into our feelings and understanding. They led us to be aware of the collective human memory hidden deep within every one of us. This archetypal memory is overlaid with all the experiences of our conscious life, which cannot reach where only our preconsciousness can gain entrance. The culture-shock which probably strikes each of us when we lose the safety of our familiar world also created the possibility of our understanding the secret language of symbols in which timeless wisdoms are contained.

The last of the seventy-eight cards painted was the Daughter of the South, the card of Isis. This card is linked to the card of the Daughter of the North, the Celtic Brigid. The Isis painting depicts the head of a woman adorned with symbols of the highest spirituality. With the image of a woman in the final painting for the cards, the essence of this Tarot deck is emphasized. From the first painting, the Wheel of Fortune, to the last, Isis, the theme is one of the common longing for a society that finds its inner harmony again—in the return to equality between man and woman. The balance between male and female energies is a necessary prerequisite for a harmonious society, though in our patriarchal world it seems almost a utopian concept.

In publishing his Tarot deck, Hermann Haindl now stands at another threshold. In this third phase of his life work, he must let go of his creations and allow them to go out into the world. In the absence of a harmonious balance, our nations will not stop destroying each other in war. Our food, the air we breathe and the earth itself will be further poisoned by a society moving away from balance. The Haindl Tarot cannot bring about significant changes in the way we all conduct ourselves. Its positive influence will be almost weightless and barely detectable.

However, there is an ever-expanding network of people who not only fend off that which is destructive, but also go further and nurture that which is spiritual. The Haindl Tarot is a part of this network. Many people will see these cards and be moved by them. In this way the rich experience and understanding captured in these inspired images will help balance the scales—with the weight of a feather.

Erika Haindl

# PAINTER'S NOTES
# AND ACKNOWLEDGMENTS

I WANT TO DEDICATE the Haindl Tarot to my wife Erika. As these cards are being published and find their way into the public, she and I will have been living together for 33 years:

$$3 \quad = \text{ The Empress}$$
$$3 + 3 = \text{ The Lovers}$$
$$3 \times 3 = \text{ The Hermit.}$$

I am especially indebted to Rachel Pollack who wrote this book. I also want to thank Günther Cherubini, who opened the door to the Tarot for me and who accompanied us, together with Barbara Meyer, to the old places in Ireland. Peter Müller deserves my written thanks for the many years of shared interests. Together with him I was allowed to live in a former Radha temple in Vrindavan, India, for a little while. Also, I want to express my appreciation for Herta and Wolfgang Biersack. They were my companions in Egypt, where I found Nut and Ra, Isis and Osiris.

I am deeply grateful to all our friends in the United States, including Regina Eastman, Brave Buffalo, Martin High Bear, Janet McCloud (Yetsi Blue), and Craig. My gratitude goes to Sandy Lofquist, too. They all opened their homes and hearts to Erika and myself, and we had many long and wonderful conversations about the American Indian world view. I thank my Native American friends who have given me much assistance for this Tarot.

My appreciation also goes out to Zoltán Szabó for his help in organizing the runes for the twenty-two Major Arcana. And thank you to my friends Joachim Faulstich, Gundula Mohr, Christine Gerhards and Thomas Petzold, who were with me during this journey into another world from the beginning. Dr. Diane Battung has enriched my understanding with her vast spiritual knowledge; for that I thank her. Gerhard Riemann, the editor of esoteric works at Knaur, who published the German editions of this book and the Tarot cards, also deserves my appreciation. Our work together developed into a friendship. This is one of the mysteries of Tarot—everything we need, we receive in abundance.

I want to thank both of my mothers and my sons. The conscious experience of being bound in time from yesterday to tomorrow is part of the understanding from which grew this Tarot. The young Emperor, rushing into life, embodies the image of the Sons, the next generation to come. As the Emperor—with the untroubled strength of his youth—becomes an enduring and understanding man throughout the course of the Major Arcana, each generation is given the room to have its own life realization.

As a part of the life circle, each of us needs not only the dialogue with himself, but also—and especially—the exchange with others. Out of the abundance of friendship and love I was allowed to receive comes my deep thankfulness, which includes also those whom I did not mention here, but who helped shape this work.

I thank the Great Spirit.

Hermann Haindl
Castagneto Carducci
1988

If you are unable to find any Newcastle book or the Haindl Tarot deck at your local bookstore, please write to:

Newcastle Publishing Co., Inc.
13419 Saticoy Street
North Hollywood, CA 91605

*The Haindl Tarot, Volume I: The Major Arcana* and *The Haindl Tarot, Volume II: The Minor Arcana* are $9.95 each, and The Haindl Tarot deck is $15.00. Please add $2.00 for UPS and handling to the cost of the book or deck for the first item ordered, plus $1.00 for each additional item. California residents please add sales tax with each order.

Free, complete, current catalogues are available upon request. Just send us your name and address and we will send you a catalogue.

Quantity discounts are available to groups, organizations and companies for any Newcastle title. Telephone (213) 873-3191 or FAX your order to Newcastle Publishing Co., Inc. at (818) 780-2007.

Thank you for your interest in Newcastle.

*AL SAUNDERS*
Publisher